ESCAPE TO
# Provence

Photography by Owen Franken
Text by Nancy Coons

**Fodor's**

FODOR'S TRAVEL PUBLICATIONS
NEW YORK • TORONTO • LONDON • SYDNEY • AUCKLAND • WWW.FODORS.COM

First Edition
ISBN 0-679-00516-1
ISSN 1528-3097

**Special Sales**

Fodor's Travel Publications are available at special discounts for bulk purchases for sales promotions or premiums. Special editions, including personalized covers, excerpts of existing guides, and corporate imprints, can be created in large quantities for special needs. For more information, contact your local bookseller or write to Special Markets, Fodor's Travel Publications, 201 E. 50th Street, New York, NY 10022. Inquiries from Canada should be directed to your local Canadian bookseller or sent to Random House of Canada, Ltd., Marketing Dept., 2775 Matheson Boulevard East, Mississauga, Ontario L4W 4P7. Inquiries from the United Kingdom should be sent to Fodor's Travel Publications, 20 Vauxhall Bridge Road, London, England SW1V 2SA.

Library of Congress Cataloging-in-Publication Data available upon request.

**Acknowledgments**

From Owen Franken: Thank you, new friend Kathie Baccala of Qualex Kodak Premium Processing in Fairlawn, New Jersey, for the wonderful treatment of my films, Kodak and otherwise. And to Heinz Niederhoff and Beatrice Geier at Kemwel Holiday Autos, for the great service and cars and for their smart idea to lease a brand-new Peugeot (instead of renting—although they do that, too). And to my wife, Annemiek, for letting me escape Paris from time to time, and to Lucien and Juliette Blanc for their gîte, their tomatoes, and their pool, which occupied my kids, Tunui and Manui, while I ran off to "Another market, dad? Do we really need more garlic?" And to Fabrizio La Rocca and the team who pulled this together.

From Nancy Coons: Many thanks to Gälle Koch at Gîtes-de-France for providing homes-away-from-home, to the tractor-driving Comtesse for her hospitality at Château de St-Martin, and to Alain Paulin at the Hôtel Hermès in Marseille for stakeout access. Thanks to Sylvie Schmitt of the Comité Départemental du Tourisme du Var and to Bernard Chouial of the Comité Départemental du Tourisme des Alpes de Haute Provence, both fonts of information and moral support. And a clink of the pastis glass to dear Christine, Christian, and Bernard Menut for letting us play shepherd for ten days, even if we did drive the sheep over the edge. Warm thanks to Fabrizio for a fruitful collaboration. And above all, loving gratitude to John and Alta for babysitting, and to Mark and Elodie and Alice—for letting me escape to Provence!

**Credits**

Creative Director and Series Editor: Fabrizio La Rocca
Editorial Director: Karen Cure
Art Director: Tigist Getachew

Editor: Jennifer Kasoff
Editorial Production: Tom Holton
Production/Manufacturing: C.R. Bloodgood, Robert B. Shields
Maps: David Lindroth, Inc.

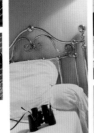

Most books on the travel shelves are either long on the nitty gritty and short on evocative photographs, or the other way around. We at Fodor's think that the different balance in this slim volume is just perfect, rather like the intersection of the most luscious magazine article and a sensible, down-to-earth guidebook. On the road, the useful pages at the end of the book are practically all you need. For the planning, roam through the color photographs up front: Each one reveals a key facet of the corner of Provence it portrays, and taken together with the lyrical accompanying text, all convey a sense of place that will take you there before you go. Each page opens up one of Provence's most exceptional experiences; each spread leads you to the quintessential places that highlight the spirit of Provence at its purest.

Some of these experiences in Provence are sure to beckon. You may yearn to sit in the dappled shade of a plane tree, to harvest olives or grapes, or simply to savor the rich aromas of loamy earth, wild lavender and thyme, wild truffles, tangy bouillabaisse. You may seek out an adventure along a clifftop trail through France's own Grand Canyon. Or learn to roast the perfect chicken in a cooking school presided over by none other than French- food guru Patricia Wells. Or bargain for antique linens in a village market. Or take in a bullfight. Or ride horseback through the Camargue marshes. You may seek shelter in a fine old auberge or retreat at day's end to a cool stone farmhouse where you gobble sweet black cherries in your very own kitchen.

To capture the magic of Provence, author Nancy Coons and photographer Owen Franken found themselves clipping grapes in the hot sun, watching the sun rise over frosty olive groves, chasing a sunset on Cézanne's Montagne Ste-Victoire, and careening across the countryside in search of the perfect borie, the ultimate lavender field. The experience, says Coons, "put me back in touch with something ancient and primordial in Provence—and maybe in myself."

It has happened to centuries of travelers before her, and it will happen to you. So be prepared to embrace the earthy richness of Provence. Forget your projects and deadlines. And escape to Provence. You owe it to yourself.

—The Editors

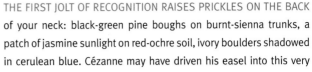

THE FIRST JOLT OF RECOGNITION RAISES PRICKLES ON THE BACK of your neck: black-green pine boughs on burnt-sienna trunks, a patch of jasmine sunlight on red-ochre soil, ivory boulders shadowed in cerulean blue. Cézanne may have driven his easel into this very soil, south of his beloved Aix-en-Provence. The highway leads into the city center and you approach the old-town streets like a pilgrim, pausing piously before his father's hat shop, his art school, the lycée where the young philosopher-painter matched wits with classmate Émile Zola. Up the deep-shaded Cours Mirabeau you follow in their footsteps to the Brasserie Les Deux Garçons—murals, oak, beveled glass—and sip espresso from a gold-rimmed cup. There are dark-visaged students here, reading, in earnest debate . . . like the inseparable Cézanne and Zola in their school days. On a hill outside the old town

# Tracing Cézanne

## AIX-EN-PROVENCE TO MONTAGNE STE-VICTOIRE

It's all there—his studio, his bric-a-brac, his oft-painted Montagne Ste-Victoire, and the brasserie where, as a young *lycéen*, he philosophized with Émile Zola.

you climb reverently, remembering weak-kneed epiphanies in art museums long ago and far away. Ascend the old oak stairs. In his studio, cool northern light emanates from the vast picture window he designed. Here, preserved in still-life as they last fell, lie familiar objects. The bowler hat, the redingote dangle casually from a peg. The ginger jar, cloudy green bottles, a scrap of china-blue cloth. Brushes, palettes smeared in color. An articulated wooden mannequin in voluptuous full-stretch . . . ah, yes, he painted *Les Grandes Baigneuses* here. In the fading light, you head to the car for a final pilgrimage eastward. Beyond the city the landscape softens and divides into patchy cubes—indigo, ochre, jade, black—and floating disembodied above rises Cézanne's most-painted subject: the Montagne Ste-Victoire. As the sun sets behind you, a painterly light show— rose, buff, pewter, cobalt—plays across a faceted surface of bisected planes, abstracted, revealed. The birthplace of Modern art, some say. And Cézanne the midwife.

Light, form, reference and resonance: From Aix and the surrounding countryside, Cézanne drew inspiration, and filled the Jas de Bouffan, his country home, with objects and artworks that later found their way to his Aix atelier. From these simple sources—evening light on pine bark, rough crockery and globes of fruit—the artist deconstructed forms and launched an abstract century.

THE SMELL HITS YOU BEFORE YOU TURN THE CORNER ONTO Carpentras's Place Aristide Briand—musky, faintly putrid, exuding bestial sensuality in the chilly winter air. No wafting smoke of roasting chestnuts here. This is a scent that lowers your eyelids, spurts saliva under your tongue, and sends you, doglike, into point: Truffles! Follow your nose to the cluster of dealers who huddle in thick coats, their steamy breath mingling with the smoke of Gitanes. A basket dangling from one arm, a leather purse from the other: It's a peculiarly Provençal blend of medieval market and back-alley drug deal. Peruse the faces before you in search of an honest man, then peer into the basket he proffers, where wrinkly black balls nestle in a plastic grocery bag. Nod, and together fade discreetly into a café where, over a glass of breakfast rosé, you discuss, sotto

# Black Gold

## TRUFFLE COUNTRY, FROM CARPENTRAS TO RICHERENCHES

*The nose knows: Sniff deep, scratch with your thumbnail, and flash your cash— discreetly, of course. Subtle and deliciously dubious, the truffle market flourishes on intrigue.*

voce, the dealer's source. His is the best truffle dog in the Enclave des Papes, he assures you, slipping snapshots of a scruffy sheepdog from his handbag. You leaf through color prints: ranks of slender oak trees, leaves chestnut-brown; the dog's muzzle plunging deep into mulchy soil, tail arced in ecstasy; a knife gently scraping back earth to reveal the brown-black-velvet prize. You offer, counter-offer, concur. The dealer weighs your purchase, and you turn over a thick wad of francs as he presses the bag into your free hand. Tuck the loot into an inner pocket and head back to the car for a pre-lunch drive into truffle country. They're out there somewhere, at the roots of rows of oaks; you can almost smell them in the sharp cold air. As you settle at your fireside table at La Beaugravière in Mondragon, your nostrils flare at the ambrosial kitchen smells—and your palate floods in anticipation of requited truffle-lust.

of sun and fun on the Côte d'Azur. Here you bask in a private rocky paradise among *calanques*, rocky finger-coves that probe into the tall white cliffs east of Marseille. There's a niche for everyone here, room to stretch out, strip down, and contemplate the postcard perspective of azure waves licking sunbleached bluffs of awesome scale. To the west lies feisty Marseille, to the east the picture-perfect fishing village of Cassis, now a gentrified pleasure port and the launching point for your excursion into Eden. Yes, you could have scrambled along the isolated clifftops to reach your cove-of-the-day, but you weren't feeling *sportif* this morning and instead hitched a ride on a Cassis cruiser. As the boat accelerates you turn your face into the astringent salt spray. Cruise into one *calanque*, then another, the pine-

# Castaway in Paradise

## THE CALANQUES BETWEEN MARSEILLE AND CASSIS

France's second biggest city seems far, far away when the sun sparkles on your personal cove, your own rocky outcrop, a stretch of beach at the end of the world.

studded cliffs towering over you, microscopic hikers clinging to the trail overhead. Along the outer bluffs nude bathers drape over sun-warmed rocks. Your ultimate destination: En Vau, the third *calanque* west of Cassis, a secluded cove with a fingernail of white beach set deep in a bluff-lined fjord. First take a swim in the jewel-toned water, then savor a sensual feast of sea urchins and chilled white Cassis. Today you are *sauvage;* tomorrow you'll dine in style at Les Goudes, the first *calanque* east of Marseille and one of the coast's best-kept secrets. Drive from the city to the coast road's dead-end, crest the last hill, and—*voilà!*—a film-set lagoon lined with restaurant tables and lounge chairs. This is the Baie des Singes, Bay of the Monkeys, so called because of the blind eye turned to passing smugglers. Deliciously illicit—what a site for a *tête-à-tête!*—it mingles the hedonistic delights of the fresh-grilled catch of the day, a nap in the sun, and a plunge in the turquoise waters.

No thatched cabanas here, no disco beat, no surf-side piña-coladas . . . only the occasional chug of a fishing boat or purr of a passing yacht, and a waiter slipping a sizzling platter of grilled fish onto your bay-view table.

THE EARLY MORNING SUNLIGHT, SCRUBBED TO CRYSTAL BY THE MISTRAL, LENDS A Maxfield Parrish gleam to the raked white cubes and Byzantine megamonuments that define Marseille's skyline. Your eyes are fixed at sea level, however, scanning the foreground of the Vieux Port, where fishing boats bob in red, yellow, and blue, masts clinking, nets dripping. Defended by the fishermen's wives, their night's catch lies before them, a menagerie of silvery sea monsters, not just twitching but swimming freely in plastic tubs: slack-chinned *galinettes*, spiny orange *rascasses*, horrific *baudroies* with bulldog jaws, serpentine *congres* writhing figure-eights. A merchant, roasted mahogany by southern sea sun, tethers your bundles of bay leaves and thyme. You're on your way to an authentic bouillabaisse, as only Marseille can make it. This ancient port town seduced the Phocaeans, the Greeks, the Romans, and an endless

# Mediterranean Melting Pot

## IN SEARCH OF THE PERFECT BOUILLABAISSE, MARSEILLE

Feisty and slightly louche in a sexy way, Marseille flaunts its sea culture in its frank and sensual fixation on fish.

stream of exotic goods flowed into its hill-framed harbor—and still does today. Wander inland up the dense city streets and lose yourself in Little Tunisia. On rue Longue-des-Capucins, the shops enfold you with a heady blend of North African colors and smells, incense-intense. Produce stands flaunt okra, twisted chili peppers, dense roots, olives round and gleaming as the jewels of Byzantium. Bright boxes of dried tamarind, orange water, coffee, couscous, fava beans stack shop windows. Inside, behind counters under lock and key, you'll find the secret, subtle ingredient that perfumes the broth with the sirocco: saffron, in tiny vials of red-ochre powder that, on contact with the fish stock, tints it instantly gold. Whether you trundle your finds home to a stockpot or follow your nose to one of the restaurants that line the ports, you're ready for the real Marseille moment: a bowl of red-gold broth, a dab of chili-spiked *rouille*, a steaming platter of last night's catch.

The streets of Marseille are one big market,
perfumed with the Fertile Crescent and the
seawinds blowing in off the Vieux Port.

Simmered in saffron and
Provençal herbs and filleted
tableside by local pros,
a great bouillabaisse draws
loyals to Chez Fonfon on the
Vallon des Auffes.

# Plane Trees, Pétanque, Pastis

## COTIGNAC, HAUT VAR

THE DEEP GREEN SHADE OF THE PLANE TREES, AS DAPPLED AS THE BARK ON THEIR MASSIVE OLD TRUNKS, creates a bower of cool tranquillity, and you—after a day of fast-track touring from perched village to castle to abbey to vineyard—succumb to the almost hypnotic calm. You pull up a café chair and take root. Can the bustle of the Côte d'Azur be only an hour away in this puttering back-country town? This is quiet Cotignac's cours Gambetta, where triple ranks of thick sycamores hum with cicadas and cafés coddle low conversation, villagers and visitors mingling in serenity. It's an unassuming oasis with a plethora of pleasant cafés disproportionate, really, to the scale of the town. There is no bustle here; no one stares, no one scolds, no one patronizes. Go ahead, speak French. You'll like as not end up in a deep discussion of local politics, and when you wave your hands to mime a delicate point you look all the more like a native. You lean forward only to tip a carafe and dribble cold water into the two fingers of yellow Pastis in your glass; it transforms itself to milky white as its level rises. Survey your fellow

The living is easy, the stakes are low, and life putters on with aplomb in this delightful backwater straight out of Pagnol.

*flâneurs*—panama hats and espadrilles, flat caps and workers' blues, a pierced eyebrow, a bare midriff—an inclusive blend, all at ease in the soporific shade. Finish your newspaper and the last anisy drops of your drink, slip your hands deep into your pockets and amble idly over to the pétanque court. They're still there: Every time you saunter by, the local club hover in clusters on the flat sand, deciphering the geometry of metal balls at their feet. Go ahead, have a go. His hand on your shoulder, a man in a jungle-print shirt guides you. Weigh the ball at your hip, lock your ankles together, bend your knees, swing and pitch. The ball arcs true and—*tock!*—cracks against your target ball. Was it the pastis that made you so relaxed, or is it the mellow Provençal ambiance of Cotignac?

GET IN TOUCH WITH YOUR INNER CALIGULA AS THE CROWD pours through the massive Roman archway into Arles's coliseum, the first-century arena where an ancient dance between man and beast is underway. Spanish culture may replace Latin, lions give way to bulls, and togas to toreador pants, but the bloodthirsty spirit remains. The mob sits silent and intent as the pageantry of the *corrida de rejón*—the horseback bullfight—unfolds in the sand. Fine-boned steeds arch delicate necks as their riders, centaur-like, tighten thighs to turn around the snorting bull, leading him in an infuriating circle dance. "E-hé, e-hé!" taunts the toreador, until he delivers the *coup de grâce*—thumbs down!—a pike to the spinal cord. The bull buckles, snorts, and collapses in the sand . . . and the masses roar like Romans. Victorious, the gladiator struts in a shower of red carnations.

# Latter-day Gladiators

## CORRIDA AND COURSES CAMARGUAISES, ARLES

ESCAPE TO PROVENCE

*Spanish roots tap deep into Roman rituals in Arles's ancient imperial coliseum, where bullfights, both bloody and bloodless, entrance fascinated crowds.*

Tonight the Latin blood pounds as the Arlésiens revel in their Spanish roots, running with bulls in the street, feasting on paella, dancing—their heels hammering at the floor, fingers snapping high over their heads. Fino sherry gives you the courage to spin with a stranger in red, eyes locked in sexual challenge—not unlike this morning's *corrida de torros,* the classic horseless bullfight between matador and bull. You wake up weary of blood-lust and buy a seat for the *courses camarguaises,* the region's genteel answer to Spanish machismo. Twenty lithe sportsmen in tennis whites try to snatch the *cocarde*—a ribbon tied to the bull's horn. Like a dog playing frisbee, the bull enters the spirit of the game, blasting steam through lowered nostrils, pawing the sand, and charging the players, who spring gracefully over the railing to safety. The ribbon won, corral gates swing wide and the bull's shoulders straighten. As the crowd roars its delirious approval, he thunders triumphantly offstage, alive, to fight again.

Some like it hot, others play it cool: Spanish-style corridas pit man against beast in a sizzling, sinister ritual of sacrifice. In the *courses camarguaises*, lithe men in sneakers romp with the bull, who chases and pounces— and lives to play again.

Hot-blooded Latins: *Feria* fever fills the streets of Arles with Spaniards-for-a-day, who don folklorique finery, feast on sherry and paella, then dance til dawn. Olé!

AS YOU DRIVE THROUGH THE ORCHARDS BENEATH THE PURPLING SHADOW OF MONT Ventoux there's a whiff of fairy tale in the air, a patchwork landscape finely drawn as a medieval illumination, luminous as an illustration in a children's book. Row after row of fruit trees—apricots, cherries, almonds—strobe past as you drive east of Orange through the vast fertile plain of the Comtat Venaissin. Once upon a time its farmlands and enviable wines—Gigondas, Vacqueyras, Beaumes-de-Venise—were hotly contested and, once won, rudely defended by a hot-blooded clan of lords. The feudal air remains: Hills rear up right and left crowned with castles, impregnable ziggurats of weathered stone above the silvery tufts of olive. A small arrow points the way to Le Barroux and on impulse you swing the wheel left, to enter a labyrinth to the past. Orchards and olive groves give way to stone, and houses, cereal-box slim, seem to

# Once Upon a Time

## LE BARROUX, MONT VENTOUX

Lose yourself in another world: Hilltowns stand aloof, setting their timeless pace to the trickling of fountains, the whisper of ivy, the scuff of espadrilles on worn stone.

grow out of the bedrock, closing in around your suddenly unwieldy car. Park by a trickling lion's-head fountain and go it on foot. Broad plane trees shade miniature squares, and mysterious alleys snake upward in every direction. You follow, past blunt Romanesque buttresses and a nail-studded church door, past sculpted fountains, past pastel-shuttered windows and weathered jars of fuchsia. A post office and an unmarked épicerie are the only signs of modern life. You climb, mesmerized, to the chateau grounds at the top and, leaning your elbows on a 12th-century wall, take in lordly views of a fairy-tale domain: First, the tile-row roofs spilling down at Cubist angles; then the vegetable patches and ancient sheepfolds; then the orchards and fields skewing pell-mell, quilting the green valley to the horizon. And, on neighboring hilltops under the protective skirts of Mont Ventoux, other strongholds of other lords, surveying coveted terrain.

IT'S A JUNE NIGHT IN CASTELLANE, THE PRE-ALPINE CROSSROADS for *sportifs*, and after a day's kayaking on the Verdon you're kicking back in a café with a well-earned mug of beer. And—what's more—there's a street festival in full swing, with local rock bands on every square, strobing color spotlights competing with yellow lanterns strung between the plane trees. But wait: As the band stops to tune, an otherworldly sound emerges in the distance. Bells . . . a cacophony of bells tonking and clunking, a deep arhythmic tintinnabulation punctuated by ear-splitting whistles and the reedy bleating of sheep. Across the street the grocer emerges from his épicerie and strains to see up the road. The baker's wife bustles out to roll in her pots of geraniums. You rise with the crowd and squeeze along the sidewalk, craning your neck. In the dim neon-

# Heading for the Hills

## THE TRANSHUMANCE, ALPES-DE-HAUTE-PROVENCE

Transhumance stems from the Latin *trans* as in transit, humance from *humus*, or earth. Thus the ancient and primeval ritual is aptly named "earth passage."

stained twilight, a row of men walks slowly abreast, as if leading a peace march. The din of thunking bells, of baaaing and beh-heh-heh-ing, rises—and a tide of sheep begins to flow past. And continues to flow, lavalike, a mass of woolly backs spreading exponentially down Main Street. The musicians gape, grab a mike, and lead the crowd in a cheer: "*Bienvenue à Castellane, la transhumance!*" It is a yearly ritual, this ancient rite of passage from the yellow-dry prairies of the Haut-Var into the succulent green pastures of the Alpes. Herds pour inexorably cross-country, wave upon wave, spanning bridges, splashing through streams, commandeering the highways in herds of 2,000 and more. They will spend the summer in the highest, juiciest alpine meadows under the watch of one lone shepherd. And then, in October, they'll return. Tonight, the wave passes, the youngest lambs scampering after their mothers' heels. The crowd listens as the gamelan fades away. And the rock band plays on.

Herd instinct: Thousands of sheep flow as one across the changing landscape, from dry lowlands to the juicy green meadows of the Alps. Dogs and man alike enjoy the ritual, trudging (and chasing) before dawn, after dark, into a world beyond.

# Trial by Trail

## HIKING THE SENTIER MARTEL, GORGES DU VERDON, ALPES-DE-HAUTE-PROVENCE

CRAB-WALK OVER RUBBLE SLIDES AND CRAWL OVER SLICK WET LIMESTONE, CLING TO THE GUIDE-rope and turn your boots to mince delicately up the chiseled bedrock steps. If you're feeling dizzy don't look down. It's a clear, unencumbered drop to the bottom, where the turquoise torrent of the Verdon snakes through this, France's own Grand Canyon, the Gorges du Verdon. You have tackled the Sentier Martel, the most spectacular and often most harrowing segment of France's renowned Grandes Randonées—with hours to go before you sleep. This canyon trail was constructed by the Touring Club in the 1930s, which blasted tunnels through cliffs and bolted railings into rock face just so intrepid hikers could penetrate where only one man had gone before—its namesake, spelunker Édouard Martel (1859—1938). Now the brave and the reckless can test their mettle on the 240 ladder-steps driven deep into cleft rock, a nearly vertical descent suspended over glorious nothingness. It's not all harrowing, of course: Long level stretches let you take your eyes off your feet and take in the magnificent

surroundings. Massive bluffs loom above, evocative grottoes sink deep into cliffs, ravens and osprey kite in eddies of canyon wind. And when the trail reaches the bottom along the way, heave off your boots, peel off your socks, and sink your battered feet into the milky green water—a swirling ice pack to cure all ills. If it's hot out, why stop there? Strip down and dive in. But bear in mind that rather unnerving sign on the bank—the desperately sprinting stick figure pursued by a blue tidal wave: Électricité de France controls the water levels and occasionally opens the flood gates. All the more adventure for you....

Keep your eyes on your feet and don't look down until you've safely scaled the ladders and slippery goat paths that thread high above the gorgeous torrent.

UNPACK THE BINOCULARS ON MONOGRAMMED LINEN SHEETS and hang the waxed jacket next to your riding boots in the halogen-lit, lavender-scented walk-in closet: Your room at the Mas de Peint, in the grassy Camargue flatlands south of Arles, strikes just the right balance between dainty elegance and rugged insouciance. A motor revs below your casement window, and you dash down stairs to the idling jeep just in time to peel out of the drive in a spray of gravel. Your driver, in plaid flannel and cowboy hat, careens down rutted trails and over the vast expanse of flatlands—rice fields, reedy marshes, prairies studded with scrub. At a barbed-wire gate, you skid to a halt. This is the bull pen, a rodeo-style ring with bleachers where your host, Jacques Bon, puts his livestock through their paces. In a cloud of dust three *gardians*—Camargue cowboys—taunt and

# Home on the Range

## MAS DE PEINT, LE SAMBUC

Gentleman rancher, self-styled cowboy, and flamboyant host to a fashionable dude ranch *à la camarguaise:* Jacques Bon preserves an eccentric way of Provençal life.

parry with a stocky bull, who tosses his horns and pounces like a jungle cat. The feisty ones, the ones with *caractère*, will go on to the arenas at Arles and Stes-Maries to run the *courses camarguaises.* But the slow learners—well, they wind up as a succulent slab of bull steak sizzled on an open fire, glittering with marsh-skimmed sea salt. Lean on a fence post and watch the culling process, then hoist yourself onto the saddled Camargue horse in the neighboring stable for a muddy trot through the marshes. Tonight, silt-splashed and leather-stained, you'll sink into a canopy-draped bathtub and dress for a candlelight dinner in the grand old ranch-house's kitchen. Resplendent in Provençal silks and velour, Jacques greets guests with his brilliant mustachioed grin; after, you adjourn to the library and, Cognac in hand, sink deep into a wingback before the stone fireplace. This, then, is Home on the Range, *à la provençale.*

Barren green flatlands, ghostly steeds: The gothic landscapes of the Camargue counterbalance firelit interiors, regional antiques and creature comforts, whether you dine in the elegant Mas de Peint country kitchen or venture up the road for a char-grilled bull steak Chez Bob.

WAKE UP WITH THE ROOSTERS AND THROW OPEN CASEMENT windows to lean out over the cool, dewy vineyards; slip on your espadrilles and stroll, the resident collie circling ecstatically around your heels, down the dusty road to the melon fields. The sous jingling in your sweat pants suffice to buy three golden globes from an early-rising field worker. Tote your trophies back to your home-away-from-home, where the coffee's dripped and ready. You carry a steaming bowl onto the terrace, slice into the juicy pulchritude of melon and, slurping, resolve: Never stay in a mere hotel again. Not when renting this cool stone farmhouse in the heart of the Luberon—two whole weeks!—lets you immerse yourself in the Provence Peter Mayle made you sigh for: The leisure to get to know the cheese lady at the local market, to stumble on village

# Living the Gîte Life

## RURAL HOLIDAY RENTAL, THE LUBERON

*Just like home, only better: Pour your own drinks, turn up the radio, cook up all those market goodies, and let the kids run barefoot.*

festivals and stay to dance, to establish a table at a favorite café, to sniff out the best rosé among the local wineries and—what the heck—buy a jug: *C'est les vacances!* Tonight you'll ease a basket of market goodies onto the kitchen table—plump eggplants, black sweet cherries, a wizened farm sausage, a fat skinned rabbit, a bundle of rosemary—and, dialing the radio to a hip-swaying samba, pour yourself a pastis from your own bottle. (You've done the mini-bar scene enough. And the square jelly packets at breakfast, the no-refills coffee, the triple-priced wine, the waiter whose nostrils flare at the smell of children. Not to mention the sprinting from sight to sight, nose glued to the guidebook, shutter-snapping-château-hopping-pedal-to-the-metal. . . .) Tonight you'll cook barefoot, eat long and late under sultry stars and carry limp children to their bedroom. You smile smugly and, stretching, rise to pour yourself a refill bowl of coffee. Another fine gîte day stretches ahead.

Kick off your shoes and finish that paperback while the kids have the run of the place—your place. Even hanging out the wash takes on a pastoral glamour during your country-house idyll.

THE APPLE-CRISP FRAGRANCE OF AUTUMN-MORNING AIR MINGLES with the musty-sour scent of new wine as you clamber onto the back of the truck, your fellow workers jostling, laughing as you roll out for the day's labors in the vineyards. Lorgues is rosé country, in the Var back-country hills far above the coast, and you are a migrant guest participating in the September ritual of the *vendange,* the harvest. The green-black vines bow under the weight of ruby-amber grapes. You vault from the truck bed and crouch, hefting a pyramid of velvety globes in your palm, lifting it to your lips to bite. A burst of sugary juice runs down your chin, already tangy with the alcohol that marks the moment to seize the day. A foreman thrusts secateurs into your sticky hand, and you fall into formation, two by two, facing off across the vines. Part the

# Autumn Bacchanalia

## CÔTES DE PROVENCE GRAPE HARVEST, LORGUES, HAUT VAR

The fruits of your labors fill a steady bucket brigade that fills, in turn, vast truckbeds heavy with pulp and juice.

broad leaves, lift, clip, drop the cluster into the black bucket, move down the row. Your pail fills quickly: *"Porteur!"* you call, and he whisks your take to the truck and dumps, fruit scudding to plump softly onto a heap of juicy purple. So goes the bucket brigade to the end of the row, then up the next and down another. At breaktime, you sprawl in a patch of mint in the shade of the ancient pollards. Back at the wine press at day's end, the truckbed tips back and the grapes rush in a heavy torrent down the chute into a seething vat of pulp. Here they will stew in their own sweet juice, drawing from the skins the soft coral shade that defines rosé. Tonight, fingers blistered and back aching, you'll bathe, slip back into white-collar mode and, slightly proprietorial, toast your labors with a misty glass of Côtes de Provence.

Camaraderie and tradition: The vendange has always brought temporary workers who relish taking part in this ancient ritual. Even aristocrats roll up their sleeves and sharpen their secateurs when it's time to pick, and laborers from all walks of life share the pleasure of a redolent mouthful of a wine made from grapes you picked yourself.

IT WAS RALPH LAUREN'S GAZILLION-AND-TWO SHADES OF OFF-white that made you burn the paint samples and dig out your vacation brochures of Roussillon. And now, here you are wiggling your toes in God's own color palette, coated to your shins in red-ochre dust, your face smudged in yellow, glowing. This is the source: the quarries and mines east of Roussillon where a rich vein of raw pigment runs like blood through the Vaucluse bedrock. Enrolled in a workshop ("Decorative Chalk Stuccos") at the Conservatoire des Ochres et Pigments Appliqués in Roussillon, you spent the morning mixing and daubing, swapping plaster recipes, styling frescoes and grotesques against an earthy background. Outdoors, a class of children reveled, hands-on, in the ruby-tinged chalk and sand. In Apt, at the Societé des Ochres de

# Luxe in Terra

## ROUSSILLON TO APT, VAUCLUSE

From the ground up: Ochre is quarried from painted-desert cliffs, then applied directly to the houses around it, creating a luminous harmony between natural and man-made beauty.

France, the roar was mesmerizing, as were the rolling clouds of mustard dust, the diabolic heat of the ovens, the epic tableau of shirtless men smeared in ruddy smut heaving 50-kilo bags into truck beds. Out of such a hell-hole, what subtlety! Michelangelo knew the magical qualities of ochre—luminous pigments absorbing and refracting light—and so, instinctively, did the Provençaux, coating their stone houses with painterly layers of vermilion and saffron, delicately nuanced, chamois-soft. In the evening, on Roussillon's place de la Mairie, where you rinse your dusty throat with rosé, the light deepens to gold. The surrounding walls metamorphose slowly from lemon to mustard to mango to melon, russet to crimson to claret, throwing into cool relief louvered shutters coated in mint-green and aquamarine, a periwinkle Citroën. And you wonder, contemplating the vivid dust on your sandals: Will a 50-kilo bag of *oxyde jaune* fit into the overhead bin?

The ochre vein yields a spectrum of subtle shades from ruby to gold that, when ground, baked and mixed with chalk, yield timeless materials to be applied in a nuanced stucco, a fresco, a weathered trompe l'oeil.

It's all in the application.
From the beginning of time
man has daubed ochre-based
pigments on his walls, an
organic expression of the
earth beneath his feet.

SKIP THE SAVORY FOOD STANDS AND TURN A BLIND EYE TO THE MODERN ARTS and crafts. That's not why you've come to this mellow silk-mill town. You're here for the Sunday antiques market that lines the canals of the Sorgue, to troll the souklike maze of stands for antiques and attic treasures heaped in tantalizing disarray: a zinc hip bath, woven-willow dough baskets, row upon row of Ricard glasses glinting in the morning sun. At your elbow, a man casts a discriminating glance through half-lenses at the stamp on a silver ladle, then shrugs: A mien of disdain is the name of the game in this Marrakech of hagglers, who quibble, counter-offer, and turn on their heel—that is, until the merchant comes around: "But today we could make you a price, Monsieur. . . ." A statuesque couple, like matched wolfhounds in head-to-toe black, preen down the row, admiring each other as much as the cloisonné. Make a pass back down the rows

# Trolling for Treasure

## SUNDAY MORNING ANTIQUES MARKET, L'ISLE-SUR-LA-SORGUE

Such a deal: What will you give for this flax nightshirt, that portrait of Oncle Émile, a matched pair of cathedral kneeling chairs?

of stands, lingering to examine each Victorian clay flower pot. With a connoisseur's air, you scoff, frown, turn them in your palm, murmur to your companion: "How much? Ah, *bon*..." then wander on. By the fountain, toddlers teeter precariously over the water's edge; young lovers read paperbacks on a park bench, her head in his lap. You forge resolutely ahead: An Art Nouveau washstand, monogrammed linens, dismembered brass beds. Another stand of flower pots, no chips this time and artfully weathered. "How much? . . . and for all eight? *Bon, d'accord.*" The merchant dimples and wraps them in yesterday's *Le Provençal,* and you count out your francs. Sold! Celebrate over a pastis at a café along the mossy waterwheels and burbling canals riddling the picturesque streets of this, the only place to be on a Sunday morning in the Vaucluse.

For some, the thrill of the hunt and
the haggle. For others, to see, be seen,
or observe the scene from a ringside table
in a shady café, armed with a crème and
the Sunday papers.

AHHHH . . . YOUR FAVORITE CAFÉ CHAIR ACROSS FROM the Palace of the Popes: just the angle to contemplate its formidable 14th-century facade, its delicious history of revelry, debauchery, sacred intrigue, and secular self-indulgence—all from the staid perspective of modern Avignon. But on this fine July day the *vieille ville*, its ancient streets usually echoing with the past, is in-your-face alive. Who are all these people? A brace of black-swathed artistes hunch over cell phones, miming kisses to colleagues across the *place*. A bevy of bohemians sprawl lazily around a guitarist while a gamine with freckles and bells on her toes circles the place with handbills. A mime springs lightly from behind a kiosk and climbs an imaginary ladder. Theater people! The Festival is in town, and every viable

# The Play's the Thing

## AVIGNON THEATER FESTIVAL

When this ancient papal stronghold lets down defenses, anything goes: From a mimed gesture and a daub of body paint to operatic costumes and sets, all the world's a stage.

venue—theaters, nightclubs, cinemas, even the street itself—becomes a stage. Tonight trendy cafés up and down medieval streets host A-list soirées, and a chic crowd surges toward the Place du Palais. As the sun sets behind the Pont d'Avignon, the great gates of the Palais swing wide onto the central courtyard, where bleachers ring a temporary stage. Slip your ticket into an usher's hand and follow him up to your folding seat. The lights dim, the broad quarried stones of the palace wall glow briefly—and the play begins. A white follow-spot, a vivid costume, the ringing diction of classical French theater. No summer-stock this, but sophisticated stuff—entrancing as opera, even with your rusty French. At midnight, dazed and transported, you emerge onto the moonlit Place du Palais and uncrumple the handbills in your pocket: A matinée tomorrow? Something avant-garde after hours? Stroll evocative alleyways toward your hotel, the streets a stage-set to your elevated thoughts. Is that a dash of theatrical swagger in your step?

THERE'S A PLEASANT, URGENT BUSTLE IN THE OLD, BEAMED FARMHOUSE kitchen—the clatter of copper pans, the sizzle of herbs in olive oil, the whir of a blender, the rhythmic *tock* of chopping knives—and a background of steady banter from your team of student chefs. "I seeded the tomatoes yesterday!" "Who cleans up the work station?" "Do I heat the pan before I sauté the zucchini?" you ask, your hair frizzling in the steam. A sunny smile, a brisk, concise reply: Patricia Wells is at home in the vine-covered hills above Vaison-la-Romaine, and you are in her country kitchen learning from the master. Celebrity author of *The Food Lover's Guide to France* and restaurant critic for the *International Herald Tribune* in Paris, at once hostess, guru, earth mother, and tour guide, she has enfolded you in her Provençal way of life. With her easy, unpretentious Midwestern

# A Food Lover's Guide

## PATRICIA WELLS'S COOKING CLASSES, VAISON-LA-ROMAINE

Chopping, trimming, basting, tasting—a cornucopia of market-fresh Provençal ingredients form an artist's palette of vivid colors for apprentice cooks.

ways, she introduces you to her butcher, invites her cheeseman to lunch, guides you deep into Côtes du Rhône caves, leads you through farmer's markets to the rosiest garlic, the juiciest asparagus. Withered figs? Then change the menu, and you find yourself back in the kitchen pitting plump local cherries. Mop your brow on your personalized apron and accept a beaded glass of the neighbor's white wine. "Okay, boys and girls, come and see the chickens!" chirps Patricia, and you gather at the courtyard bread oven to ooh and aah at the sight of plump fowl sputtering gold in a copper roasting pan. At last, *à table:* in the shade of a broad, ancient live oak, a bright Provençal-print cloth adorns the groaning board where you'll savor the rewards of your labors and gaze over Patricia's private Chanteduc vineyards. She has indeed made you feel at home in her beloved Provence.

Almost as much as for access to her culinary insight, food lovers beat a path to Vaison for the privilege of a peek at Patricia Wells's dream life: an artfully restored Provençal country house, lush gardens and private vineyards, weekly ventures to the local market, long-term relations with the best butchers, bakers, vintners and cheesemakers.

Easygoing intimacy and
an enthusiasm for fresh,
unpretentious food bond
students and professor for
a week of exploration,
of application, and above
all appreciation *à table*,
where the farewell feast
is consumed alfresco against
a tapestry of bright sun,
soft shade and the croaking
of cicadas.

# Noël, Noël!

## CHRISTMASTIME, AUBAGNE

ESCAPE TO PROVENCE

YOU'VE BEEN FEELING GRINCHY ALL DAY, THE IRON WIND WHIPPING THROUGH THE LEAFLESS PLANE trees, the smell of roasting chestnuts mingling with bus fumes. Who talked you into Christmas in Provence, anyway? Nothing but mistrals, Muzak, and those kitschy little clay figurines . . . what are they called anyway? *Santons*. You wander from *santonnier* stand to stand on the cours Foch, your collar hunched against the cold. Humbug. And then: The Christmas lights come on. Suddenly the bleak blue-black late afternoon is transformed into a golden glow of garlands, stars and—the quintessential sign of a Provençal winter—yellow bulbs strung between the plane trees. Suddenly the vast nativity scene in the square's center, just so many costumed Barbies a moment before, takes on a warmth and a tender realism. Suddenly you see the brush-stroke twinkle in the clay baker's eye, the donkey's fine lashes, the headline on Papie's *Le Provençal*. And, reflected in the display glass, the eyes of the child beside you, luminous, saucer-wide. Is that a glimmer of holiday spirit stirring in your breast? Wander into the

old-town labyrinth, down a narrow alley draped with laundry and stars, and peer through a window. Gepetto-like, a man works at his bench, long, strong fingers pressing clay into molds, his colleague painting heavenly blue on rank upon rank of miniature Marys. At the hilltop, the town lights glittering below, step through the Église Saint-Sauveur's Baroque portal. Yes, there are shepherds kneeling before herald angels, and all the lead players—Mary, Joseph, ox and ass. But like Brueghel's Icarus, who fell from the sky unnoticed by indifferent peasants, behind the nativity scene a miniature Provençal life goes on—the goat herd, the woodgatherer, the buxom baker's wife, and the ebullient town fool. This touches you as no kitsch-crèche could—quirky, earthy, with deep southern roots. Maybe you'll stay for the Christmas Eve mass. . . .

Through a child's eyes, the world of the santons comes to life in crèches all across Provence—not just the Christmas story, but the tableau of quirky village life in times gone by.

IN THE ROSY EARLY MORNING LIGHT YOU HEAR ONLY THE CREAKING of the leather saddle, the soughing of the horse whose broad, muscular back steams and shifts beneath you as he plods across the salt flats. A trio of herons erupts from a stand of black-green parasol pines, flapping on slow pterodactyl wings. This is why you got up so early, hauling on boots, gulping a scalding espresso in the timbered dining hall of the Mas de Cacharel: to see the Camargue at dawn, primeval and virgin-pure, the last gasp of the Rhône as it seeps over the delta into the sea. The words of the Provençal poet Frederic Mistral echo in your ears: *Ni arbre, ni ombre, ni âme*—neither tree nor shade nor a soul—apt description of this barren, evocative landscape. With binoculars, you scan the vast, bleak ricelands in the distance as a flock of flamingoes soars toward the coast. A nutria

# The Wild, Wild Wetlands

## THE CAMARGUE MARSHLANDS, RHÔNE DELTA

Eerie stillness, silver light: Man only has squatters' rights to these eternal tidal flats, where seabirds and horses mingle in a salty demimonde, half land, half sea.

scuttles through the reeds; ducks shoot like buckshot from the canal as your horse splashes heavily through. You come upon a pair of dappled white mares, whose strong backs and long lashes match your own mount's. These are the famous horses of the Camargue, a hardy indigenous breed traced to Paleolithic times. A blurry mass of split hoofprints in the mud leads east, toward the red rising sun, and as you approach you hear the moaning bellows of the herd: Bulls, furry-black and bantam-scaled, regard you from a distance, heads swiveled toward you as one, skittish even in their stillness. Here in the free-range wilderness it's hard to remember they're private property, branded, trained, sold. Back in your whitewashed room you gaze out at the marshy horizon and wonder at the curious symbiosis of nature and nurture that is the Camargue—*la nature favorisé*.

IN THE FROST-CRISPED VALLEY, STILL PLATINUM-WHITE BEFORE the sun first slants buttery rays over the edge of the jagged Alpilles, row on row of olive trees shimmer, each ephemeral, feminine puff of silver-green a circle of six slender trees, leaning outward like dancers in a ring, tipping faces to the light. Their pale green weeping-willow tresses hang heavy with cabochon jewels—onyx, jade, amber—and, like handmaidens, you and your mittened colleagues stand tenderly combing the bejeweled fronds in your left hand, a thick-tined rake in your right. The olives drop heavily to the ground spread with net, whose edges you gather, tipping the fruit into crates. As the sun floods the valley in delicate gold—first the limestone cliffs, then the treetops, then the old stone *mas* with its tendril of rising wood smoke—you heft the crates onto the truckbed and head into

# Earth's Elixir

## LA VALLÉE DES BAUX OLIVE HARVEST, LES ALPILLES

Hand-combed from the branches in the crisp winter air, Les Baux olives have withered in the mistral winds to yield all the more oil.

Maussane. Take your place in line: Farmers from every direction are bringing their harvest to the mill, the Coopérative Oléicole de la Vallée des Baux. Keep count as your crates are emptied into a conveyor that shoots the masses of fruit into vast attic bins, where they ferment a bit—three to six days—before gushing into the mill downstairs. Here four great granite wheels grind and turn, turn and grind a mass of black pulp that oozes green-gold. Breathe deep: The oily steam coats your skin, soothes your nostrils with a rich, palpable perfume. The unctuous pulp spreads onto woven *escourtins,* permeable mats stacked into a cylinder that, when compressed in a vise-grip, gushes forth liquid gold. This, then, is the elixir that glints in the bottle on your white-linened table at lunch in all its bare-boned elegance—pure, undiluted, unembellished. Drizzle a bead of topaz-green on a chunk of bread and bite. . . .

Harvested from a handful of private farms, then pooled at the Maussane Cooperative, truckloads of plump olives are fermented, then crushed under vast granite mill wheels—and the essence of the matter drizzled, unfiltered, over lunch.

YOU FIRST MEET MONIQUE CLAESSENS AT HER MARKET stand in Forcalquier, clear-eyed and serene before a boggling array of bottles, jars, and sachets. Her massage creams, infusions, and essential oils wink like jewels in the morning sun. What better gifts to capture the painterly purples and heady aroma of the lavender fields you have crossed throughout Haute-Provence? Sated with the strong scent of souvenir soaps and sachets in folkloric fabrics, you peer at the hand-lettered labels on her essential oils—*Lavandula vera,* true wild lavender. She passes a vial of elixir under your nostrils and you close your eyes: A cool, soft mountain meadow breeze floats out of the bottle, pungent-sweet. This, then, is the essence of the stuff—the wild, pure-blood ancestor of the commercial hybrid lavender that flows in tame rows over summer hillsides, that packs

# The Essence of the Matter

## CUTTING WILD LAVENDER, ABOVE FORCALQUIER

*With wild lavender carpeting the hillsides and cultivated lavender striping the fields, the late-July blooming period dyes Provence deep purple, sweet-scented and soothing to the eye.*

the gift-shop potpourris. Come morning, you take your tiny vial from your bedstand, whiff again, and grab the car keys, knocking the guidebook to the floor. Forget sightseeing: To the source! Shift down to third and squeal around backroad curves, deep into hills corduroyed in lilac, amethyst, mauve. Stop briefly at a *borie*, wade into the ochre rows and listen to the wraparound roar of sucking bees. Onward and up an improbably steep, rocky drive; abandon the car and climb. High above Ybourgues, over a cluster of communal dwellings—17 gentle zealots pursuing a better life—you find her hip-deep in purple. There's a linen sheet crisscrossed over her shoulders, the old way, leaving a deep pouch over her hips "like a bee that carries his pollen," Monique explains. Her sickle encircles a burst of lavender flower-spikes, she clenches them into a tight pack and— *sshhhhkkk!*—slices through the stems. *Voilà!*—into the bulging sack, a dense bouquet of violet perfume-in-the-making.

YOU REALLY MUST STOP GETTING SIDETRACKED THIS WAY. . . . there are châteaux to tour, museums, Roman ruins. And yet, as the country road narrows through a village's main street, there's another row of sheltered booths, another tent draped with banners of Provençal fabric, another jumble of hand-woven baskets. Fight a brief inner battle: The back seat is already full of cherries, there's a melon rolling around in the trunk, and you're planning a four-course two-star lunch. But . . . you brake despite yourself to putter happily once again through a Provençal market. It's a daily occurence here, passed from village to town—Sunday Coustellet, Monday Cavaillon, Tuesday Vaison, Wednesday St-Rémy, Thursday Roussillon, Friday Pertuis, Saturday Apt—yet each takes on a character of its own. At Aubagne, blue-aproned *paysannes* with gnarled fingers

# A Moveable Feast

## PROVENÇAL MARKETS

Go ahead and squeeze, sniff, hand-pick the best: Marketing in Provence is a sensual, hands-on experience, tempting and tingling all five senses.

scoop a home-picked mix of mesclun; at Aix young pros in Prada pick over a boutique-style collection of olives; at Coustellet an entrepreneurial farmer in workers' blues hawks sheep manure for your vegetable patch; at La Motte merchants string night-lanterns under the cherry trees. Everywhere a procession of products marches through the seasons: fat purpling stalks of asparagus in April, strawberries ruby to the core in June, melons splitting with ripeness in July, blood-red tomatoes in September . . . and always the sausages, the herbs, the ropes of garlic, lavender soaps, India-print cottons, stacks of ceramic casseroles. But today a surprise awaits: Is that a fife and drum? You've caught Allemagne in its autumn *fête du Patrimoine*, a mix of folklore and nostalgia. Up the main street dances a miniature parade of Pagnol characters—men in velour vests, ladies in fine challis shawls and quilted print skirts—smiling proudly, self-consciously in the finery they unpacked from the attic just for today. It's all part of the daily pageant of the Provençal market.

You can bargain and
banter and taste from
Provence's rich cornucopia
of fruits, vegetables, oils
and cheeses—and then buy
the pots to simmer them
in, the plates and linens
to serve it on, and the
clothes to wear, too.

# All the Details

Now that your appetite is whetted for a Provençal escape, it's time to tackle the nuts-and-bolts of trip preparation. We've broken down by region the who, what, when, and where for each escape, as well as suggesting lodging and sightseeing in the vicinity. Prices reflect the full range within a category throughout the year (exchange rate at press time: 6.66 francs/1.05 euros to the U.S. dollar). Properties are open year-round, accept credit cards, and have private baths in-room, unless otherwise stated. When writing, remember to add "France" to the address; when phoning or faxing, dial 011-33, then the number, not including the initial zero. There's often no one who speaks English in places off the beaten track, so written requests for information or a reservation work best, phrased as simply as possible and faxed; the many Web sites given here should help.

If you fly into Paris, consider a connecting flight to Marseille's airport at Marignane. The TGV will bring you to Avignon from Paris in 3½ hours, but to really escape—that is, get involved in the real Provence—you'll want to rent a car from one of the major arrival points (Avignon, Marseille, or Aix). High summer in Provence—July and August—is overrun with tourists and very, very hot, even on the coast. Consider spring or fall to experience the mellowest climate and café life. Off-season finds a majority of resort-area hotels closed, and many restaurants too; but those that remain open are full of locals, relaxing before the summer people arrive.

## THE CAMARGUE

The Camargue, a broad delta of silt and salt that fans between the final split of the Rhône as it pours into the Mediterranean, has a peculiar ecosystem all its own and a culture—wild, quirky, isolated—just as unique. Kerchiefed cowboys called *gardians* roam the range on sturdy dappled-white horses, prodding prong-horned bulls with bloodlines that predate the cave paintings of Lascaux. Flamingoes and herons mince one-legged through rice paddies and nutria scuttle through the reeds. It's a curious symbiosis of wilderness and civilization, with all the lands privately owned but government-protected, with controlled cultivation and extremely limited tourist access. Every "wild" horse belongs to a *manadier* (rancher), and many landowners rent their marshlands out to hunters to finance the dredging and fencing required to keep the delicate ecosystem from oozing slowly toward the encroaching sea.

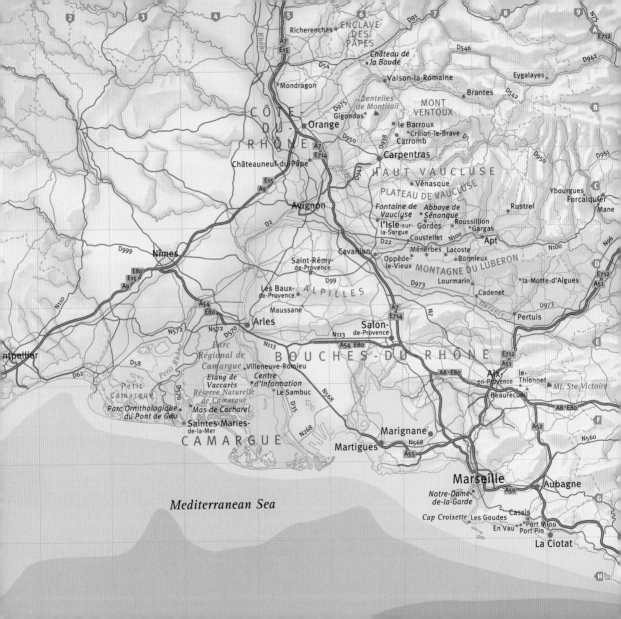

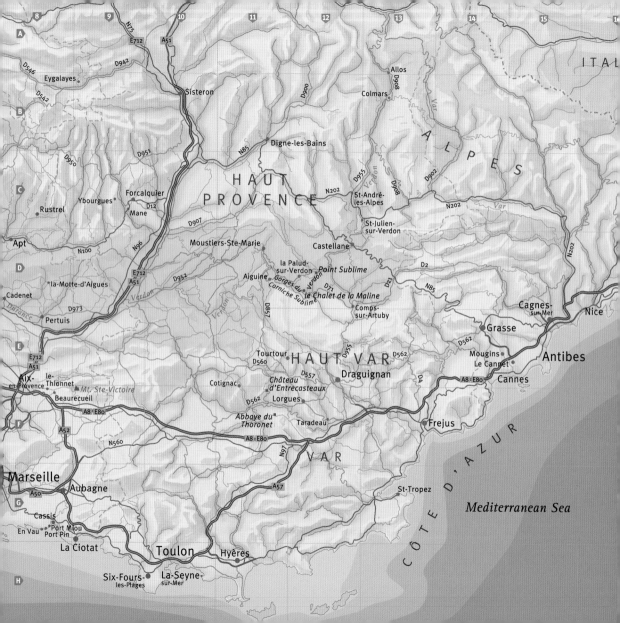

## MAS DE CACHAREL, STES-MARIES-DE-LA-MER (4F)
*The Wild, Wild Wetlands, p. 66*

This row of whitewashed rooms, with quarry-tile floors, jute rugs, and plain cotton bed throws, first knew the modern conveniences of electricity in 1968. The point here is not grand comfort but rather what you see out your window: a broad sweep of horizon, waving reeds, and fluttering egrets as far as the eye can see. This 70-hectare private estate, passed down for generations in the Colomb-de Daunant family, lies entirely within the bounds of the Parc Régional de Camargue, and most of the land borders the inner sanctum of the Réserve Naturelle de Camargue. The rustic lodge, where you eat breakfast or a platter of local cold cuts in front of the vast fireplace, was built in the 1970s of old stone and beams. Overlooking the landscape, the pool is protected from the mistral winds with plate-glass shields. This is the perfect departure point for a visit to the Petit Camargue (F3), the isolated, wind-swept dunes just west of the Petit Rhône. Or take an all-day horseback ride into the inner sanctum of the Étang de Vaccarès, where no cars may pass and only marshy trails weave through the wilderness.

**CONTACT** Hôtel de Cacharel, F-13460 Stes-Maries-de-la-Mer, tel. 04–90–97–95–44, fax 04–90–97–87–97, e-mail to mail@hotel-cacharel.com, on the Web at www.hotel-cacharel.com.

**DISTANCES** 4 km north of Stes-Maries, 37 km southwest of Arles.

**FACILITIES** 15 rooms. Bar/breakfast lodge, pool. Cold meats and picnic boxes on request.

**PRICES** Doubles 672 frs, including breakfast.

**OPTIONS** The Hôtel de Cacharel rents Camargue horses by the hour (115 frs), half-day (240 frs), or day (380 frs), always accompanied by a *gardian*. Box lunches 70 frs. If you are not a seasoned rider, opt for a short run of one or two hours.

## CORRIDA AND COURSES CAMARGUAISES, ARLES (4E)
*Latter-day Gladiators, p. 24*

Though Arles itself was never officially under Spanish rule, something of that hot-blooded culture has seeped over from the neighboring Languedoc. Arles was, on the other hand, firmly under the iron fist of Roman rule for centuries, and the two cultures marry brilliantly in the tradition of the bullfight. Within the nearly perfectly preserved 1st-century Roman coliseum the Latin ritual of man-versus-beast is played out before international crowds. The two very different forms of bullfighting coexist in Arles, with the Spanish fight-to-the-death *corrida* (and horseback *rejón*) importing toreadors from an international talent pool. This is not for the faint of heart: Six bulls are killed per *corrida,* their ears and tails awarded like Michelin stars to the best matadors. At opposite spiritual poles, the Camargue-style bullfights are not fights at all but rather games, and the clean-cut, sneaker-clad players enjoy a skillful give-and-take with the bull. Both sports are part of the *ferias,* the city-wide festivals that give the Arlésiens yet another fine excuse to trot out their Provençal finery. The biggest is the Feria de Pacques, with *corridas* and bull-running all Easter weekend. The Fête d'Arles, a series of parties, parades, and bullfights from mid-June to July, rivals the Feria for pageantry. *Courses camarguaises* are played in the arena year-round.

**CONTACT** Arles Office du Tourisme, 43 boulevard de Craponne, 13200 Arles, tel 04–90–18–41–20, fax 04–90–18–41–29.

**DISTANCES** 40 km from Avignon, 30 km from Nîmes.

**OPTIONS Hôtel Nord-Pinus:** To get in the Hemingway spirit, stay at this fashionable Place du Forum inn with a J. Peterman sense of fantasy. Kilims, oil jars, wrought iron, and jewel-tone ceramics create a stage-set for Latin romance. The bar, with its *corrida* memorabilia—matador suit, bull's head—is the only place for a sherry after the fights. Place du Forum, 13200 Arles, tel. 04–90–93–44–44, fax 04–90–93–34–00. 19 rooms, 5 suites. Brasserie, bar. Doubles 840–990 frs, suites 1,700 frs. **Hôtel Le Cloître:** Much simpler rooms in a setting that's *sympa* (friendly) can be found at this hotel behind the cloisters of St-Trophime. The owners have renovated it stone by stone and decked it with hand-rubbed ochre and Provençal cottons. 16 rue du Cloître, 13200 Arles, tel. 04–90–96–29–50, fax 04–90–96–02–88. 30 rooms. Doubles 270–390 frs.

### MAS DE PEINT, LE SAMBUC (5F)
*Home on the Range, p. 38*

Everything is larger than life at this, the ultimate Camargue dude ranch. The bull's head and yokes in the hall, the massive furniture, even the mustache over Jacques Bon's grin are all created on a grand scale, broad gestures of the masculine grace that defines this sophisticated rural retreat. There are linen sheets monogrammed with the ranch brand, baldaquin curtains draped over the four-legged tub, a cart of self-service Armagnacs by the wingbacks before the roaring fire. And dinner is served in the kitchen—not a roaring industrial workspace but a gracious, candlelit space where the house products (nutty rice, garden greens, young bull) are featured.

**CONTACT** Hôtel Le Mas de Peint, Le Sambuc, 13200 Arles, tel. 04–90–97–20–62, fax 04–90–97–22–20, e-mail to peint@avignon.pacwan.net, on the Web at www.ila-chateau.com/manade/.

**DISTANCES** 20 km south of Arles via D36.

**FACILITIES** 8 rooms, 3 suites. Restaurant, bar, pool.

**PRICES** Doubles 1,195–1,455 frs, suites 1,830–2,050 frs. Special weekly rates. Half-board (breakfast and dinner) by the week only. Breakfast 90 frs.

**OPTIONS** *Gardian*-accompanied horseback tours of the Mas de Peint's 1,250 acres should be arranged the day before (125 frs per hour). A four-wheel-drive tour of the grounds (125 frs per hour) includes a visit to the bull-breaking rodeo ring. You'll want to slip away for a lunch at **Chez Bob's**, 11 km up the backroads behind the inn. In a smoky, isolated stone cottage you'll eat what Bob's serving—anchoïade (crudités with anchovy vinaigrette), homemade duck pâté, and the pièce de résistance: a thick, sizzling slab of bull steak grilled

in the roaring fireplace. The daily fixed-price menu is 170 frs, not including wine. Villeneuve Romieu, 13200 Arles, tel. 04–90–97–00–29, fax 04–90–96–69–17.

### CAMARGUE HIGHLIGHTS

**Arles** itself is the obvious focal point of a visit to the Camargue region, with its myriad museums and Roman monuments. The state-of-the-art Musée de l'Arles Antique (Museum of Classical Arles) illustrates the city's noble history as the Rome of the north. Visit the Roman monuments, from the theater to the arena to the Alyscamps, where the Romans buried their dead. The quirky Muséon Arlaten was created by the turn-of-the-20th-century poet Frédéric Mistral, who loved and wrote of the Camargue and single-handedly sparked the revival of its Provençal culture. Église St-Trophime—especially its 12th-century portal—is one of the best-preserved and most floridly detailed works of Romanesque architecture in France.

## THE ALPILLES

East of Arles and due south of Avignon there rises a rough, rocky range of white-limestone hills, their windswept, arid isolation slashed by green-black cypress and softened by feathery, silver-green olive orchards. To many this is the heart of Provence, anchored socially by discreet, ultra-chic St-Rémy, its leisurely market-town ways serving an elite clientele of summer-*mas* owners (including Caroline of Monaco); and anchored touristically by the spectacular hilltop fortress of Les Baux, one of the most visited sites in France. Converted-*mas* hotels offer luxurious lodgings, poolside bars, and often extraordinary regional cuisine—all within an easy hour's drive of Avignon, Arles, Aix, or the Luberon. Van Gogh painted sunflowers and olive groves from his asylum in St-Rémy the year before he died, lauding the extraordinary colors and light; the Provençal poet Frédéric Mistral called the mountain range "a veritable panorama of glory and of legends."

## LA VALLÉE DES BAUX OLIVE HARVEST, MAUSSANE (5E)

*Earth's Elixir, p. 68*

Since the Greeks first brought their gift-of-the-gods to Provence some 2,500 years ago, the olive tree has taken to this mountainous landscape as if it were the slopes of an Aegean island—to which it bears more than passing resemblance. Here thrives the well-known artisanal olive mill, the Moulin Jean-Marie Cornille at Maussane, where the fruits of the orchards that pepper the Alpilles are amassed and pressed into a consistently delicious artisanal olive oil, grouped under the title La Vallée des Baux. Throughout the region, independent growers hand-pick their harvest and carry it to the Maussane mill to be crushed under the granite wheels. What they don't keep for their families is sold at the moulin sales counter, whether in curvaceous gift bottles or in sturdy industrial *bidons* (jugs). From November through mid-February, the mill wheels turn, and across the Alpilles countryside orchards are thronging with pickers, with their signature A-frame ladders, their yellow rake-shaped combs, and the froth of green net draped at the base of the olive trees. On December 10 *la baptême* (baptism) launches the new unfiltered oil, still foggy with fresh residue that will settle over the year, its powder of fruit and stone flavoring the oil as it sinks to the bottle's bottom.

**CONTACT** Moulin Jean-Marie Cornille, rue Charloun-Rieu, 13520 Maussane-les-Alpilles, tel. 04–90–54–32–37, fax 04–90–54–30–28. Sales all year Monday through Saturday 8 to noon and 2 to 6.

**DISTANCES** 31 km south of Avignon, 20 km northeast of Arles.

**OPTIONS Oustau de Baumanière**: At the foot of the hilltown of Les Baux and 5 km north of Maussane, this gastronomic landmark offers luxurious lodgings in a serene setting of manicured boxwood, rosemary, and laurel. 13520 Les Baux, tel. 04–90–54–33–07, fax 04–90–54–40–46, e-mail to office@oustaudebaumaniere.com, on the Web at www.oustaudebaumaniere.com. 13 rooms, 9 suites. Doubles 1,300–1,450 frs. Suites 2,000–2,100 frs. **Le Cabro d'Or**: Its slightly less expensive cousin, under the same management, nestles lower in the valley in a bucolic mass of rosebushes. 13520 Les Baux, tel 04–90–54–33–21, fax 04–90–54–45–98, e-mail to cabro@relaischateau.fr, on the Web at www.relais-chateaux.fr/cabro. 23 rooms, 8 suites. Doubles 650–1,100 frs. Suites 1,300–1,700 frs. **La Petite France**: For an extraordinary Provençal meal featuring local wines and the olive oil pressed at the Maussane mill just up the road, have lunch in this 18th-century former bakery in Paradou (tel. 04–90–54–41–91). Fixed-price menus are 175–260 frs. Closed Wed., no lunch Thurs.

### LES ALPILLES HIGHLIGHTS

The 11th-century fortifications of **Les Baux** (5D) loom above the olive groves, nearly indistinguishable from the naturally crenellated cliffs. One narrow main street leads visitors up through the medieval village, now lined with boutiques, and delivers them to the Château des Baux at the top. Here, on this eagle's-nest plateau, stand the ruins of a once magnificent fortress. A small museum illustrates the village's history. **St-Rémy** (5D) features two extraordinarily well-preserved Roman monuments, known simply as Les Antiques, dating from the time of Caesar Augustus. Across the road stands Glanum, the remains of an entire Greek village later taken over by the Romans, now a maze of foundations, towers, and broken columns.

# AVIGNON

Wrapped in crenellated walls with Gothic arrow slits and crowned by the massive double-palace of the rebel popes, Avignon is well fortified against modern times. It could easily have become a living museum for tourists and let life pass it by. Yet of all the cities in Provence it seems to beat with the most contemporary pulse, with its trendy cafés, cutting-edge galleries, adventuresome nightlife, and stylish boutiques. There's a thriving Les Halles marketplace, as well as sophisticated restaurants and esoteric museums. All this creative energy bubbles inside a thick stone stronghold of romantic, timeless beauty, reflected in the steady, imperturbable Rhône.

## AVIGNON THEATER FESTIVAL/FESTIVAL D'AVIGNON (5C)

*The Play's the Thing, p. 58*

While this medieval city is most accessible in spring and fall, when the mellow rhythm of café-and-market life is in full swing, Avignon is at its most scintillating and urbane during the last two weeks of July, when its time-honored theater festival takes the city by storm. There are two official festivals, with the more avant-garde and/or smaller-budget productions combining under the title "Off." Send for pre-programs in March and order tickets on receiving the final program and ticket package in May (don't delay!). The prestigious, big-budget showpiece every year is featured in the *cour d'honneur,* the courtyard of the Palace of the Popes itself. Yes, the productions are in French, but even if your skills aren't at Académie Française level you'll find the magic of theater weaves its spell. You'll have to book lodging far in advance to stay in the city.

**CONTACT** For more information about the festival, contact the Association de Gestion du Festival d'Avignon, 8 bis rue de Mons, 84000 Avignon, tel. 04–90–27–66–50, fax 04–90–27–66–83. Paris headquarters: 6 rue de Braque, 75003 Paris, tel. 01–44–61–84–84, fax 01–44–61–85–27. These Web sites also offer helpful information: www.festival-avignon.com, www.avignon-off.org, and www.chartreuse.org.

**DISTANCES** 84 km west of Marseille, 31 km south of Orange.

**OPTIONS Hôtel de la Mirande:** To experience extravagance worthy of Avignon's popes, book rooms at this magnificent former cardinal's palace at the foot of the Palais des Papes. Restored and embellished with sumptuous fabrics and deluxe bathrooms, it's the perfect setting for a theatrical séjour in Avignon. There's a fine restaurant, from which diners gaze up at palace walls that are illuminated in summer. Pl. de la Mirande, 84000 Avignon, tel. 04–90–85–93–93, fax 04–90–86–26–85. 19 rooms, 1 suite. Restaurant, bar, air-conditioning. Festival rates: doubles 1,850–2,600 frs, suite 3,700 frs. Book early—even before Easter—to be sure of a room. **Hôtel de Blauvac:** More modest lodgings at the heart of the old town can be found at this 17th-century townhouse

replete with aged oak and stone. 11 rue de la Bancasse, 84000, Avignon, tel. 04–90–86–34–11, fax 04–90–86–27–41. 16 rooms. Bar. Doubles 425 frs, 40 frs breakfast.

### AVIGNON HIGHLIGHTS

The must-see in Avignon is, of course, the Palais des Papes, the vast 14th-century stronghold created to defend and coddle the popes who abandoned Rome for a new northern church-empire. Once lavish, its decor was stripped during the Revolution, and what remains has an almost monastic purity. Across the Place du Palais, the superb bijoux art museum in the Petit Palais contains an extraordinary collection of Renaissance Italian art. And don't miss the Pont St-Bénézet, the bridge in the famous children's song "Sur le pont d'Avignon, on y danse tous en rond." It still stretches over the Rhône, but only halfway; the other half was washed away in the 17th century.

# HAUT VAUCLUSE

To the north and east of Avignon the earth rises gently from the Rhône toward the formidable Mont Ventoux, the broad, looming monolith that lords over the fertile Comtat Venaissin (County of Venasque). At its foot, stone hilltowns perch over the valley, guarding this long-coveted land. What made it so desirable to the Counts, the Popes, and innumerable feudal lords? Just what makes it desirable to visitors today: *la gastronomie.* Gourmets and gourmands make pilgrimages to this region to savor its apricots, cherries, and plums; to melt over candy crunchy with local almonds; to inhale the musky perfume of truffles rooted out of surrounding oak groves. The art of aging goat cheese drifts down from the Drôme to the north. And the wines are worthy of a papal empire: Châteauneuf-du-Pape, named for the anti-pope's country house north of Avignon; the muscular Côtes-du-Rhône Gigondas and Vacqueyras; and Beaumes-de-Venise, renowned for its almond-perfumed sweet Muscat.

## TRUFFLE COUNTRY, FROM CARPENTRAS TO RICHERENCHES (6A–C)

*Black Gold, p. 12*

From the foot of Mont Ventoux to the Rhône and into the fertile Enclave des Papes (a circle of Vaucluse territory once isolated by the Avignon popes well north of the bulk of the Vaucluse), mulchy oak groves incubate one of the most sought-after culinary treasures in the world, known as *la truffe noire du Périgord*. Markets at Carpentras (6C) and Richerenches (6A), in the Enclave, draw chefs and food-industry suppliers and discerning home cooks from around the world to bargain and buy truffles, whether one at a time or in bulk. Costing from 4,000 to 5,000 frs per kilo, with each weighing from 90 to 200 grams, they inspire serious negotiation. Watch out for shady deals, including truffles weighted with buckshot, caked with mud, or painted black.

**CONTACTS** The truffle market at Carpentras runs every Friday morning mid-November through February on the Place Aristide Briand and in the Café de l'Univers. The Richerenches truffle market runs every Saturday morning during the season on the main street and in the Café Le Provençal. For more information, contact the Carpentras Office du Tourisme, 170 allée Jean-Jaurès, 84200, tel. 04–90–63–00–78, fax 04–90–60–41–02.

**DISTANCES** Carpentras is 24 km northeast of Avignon. Richerenches is 33 km north of Orange.

**OPTIONS La Beaugravière:** The firelit restaurant at Mondragon (17 km northwest of Orange) is an institution in the truffle world, with chef Guy Jullien preparing a vast array of dishes based on this coveted fungus. Local lamb and rabbit are featured, as well as an encyclopedic selection of Rhône wines. Route Nationale 7, 84430 Mondragon, tel. 04–90–40–82–54. **Hôtel du Fiacre:** For lodging some 400 meters from the Carpentras market, try this renovated 18th-century convent with a garden courtyard and modest but comfortable rooms. 153 rue Vigne, 84200, tel. 04–90–63–03–15, fax 04–90–60–49–73. 18 rooms, 2 suites. Doubles 290–480 frs, suites 450–480 frs. Breakfast 40 frs.

## PATRICIA WELLS'S COOKING CLASSES, VAISON-LA-ROMAINE (6B)

*A Food Lover's Guide, p. 60*

Patricia Wells is the only American ever to have worked as a restaurant critic for a French publication. The magnitude of this achievement can only be understood when you know the French, whose presumption of global authority and exclusive franchise on the subject of food allows little more than a dismissive shrug for foreigners—and especially foreigners from the *pays du MacDo*. Her incisive judgement, enthusiasm, and determined sleuthing—both for her books *The Food Lover's Guide to Paris* and *The Food Lover's Guide to France,* and for her restaurant column in the Paris-based *International Herald Tribune*—have won her a loyal following. Now, Wells has leveraged her considerable reputation with the considerable charm of her adopted Provence, and offers seven weeks of cooking classes at her farmhouse in Vaison-la-Romaine. Their title—"At Home with Patricia Wells: Cooking in Provence"—says it all. Only eight students per week may participate. A special four-day truffle workshop immerses students in the local truffle culture and includes a visit to a truffle-oil processing plant.

**CONTACT** Deborah Orrill, 7830 Ridgemar Dr., Dallas, TX 75231, fax 214/343–1227, e-mail to cookingclasses@patricia wells.com, on the Web at www.patriciawells.com.

**DISTANCES** 30 km northeast of Orange, 28 km north of Carpentras.

**PRICES** The price for a week's class is $3,000 per student, including all meals but not lodging. Reservations must be confirmed 120 days in advance with a down payment of $1,000. The four-day truffle workshop costs $3,000. Book as soon as possible, as spaces fill up quickly.

**OPTIONS Château de la Baude:** Six km northwest of Vaison, this miniature fortress of a farm offers bed-and-breakfast accommodations, including two suites. La Baude, 84110 Villedieu, tel. 04–90–28–95–18, fax 04–90–28–91–05, e-mail to labaude@pacwan.fr. 4 rooms, 2 suites. Pool, whirlpool, tennis court. Doubles 580 frs, duplex for 4 people 880, including breakfast. **Hostellerie Le Beffroi:** Perched on the hilltop in Vaison's old town, this splendid 16th-century house has been transformed into a small hotel. Ask for one of the big corner rooms with a view. Rue de l'Evêché, 84110 Vaison la Romaine, tel. 04-90-36-04-71, fax 04-90-36-24-78. 22 rooms. Restaurant, pool. Doubles 465–655 frs. Closed mid-Feb.–mid-Mar. and mid-Nov.–mid-Dec.

### LE BARROUX, MONT VENTOUX (6B)
*Once Upon a Time, p. 30*

Le Barroux has guarded the Comtat Venaissin since the 12th century, its thick, round towers watching over the plush green valleys as well as the jagged hills known as the Dentelles de Montmirail. Passed from one feudal lord to another, then taken over by the Avignon popes, it was "liberated" by the Revolution in 1791—first sacked, then reclaimed for France. It won't take you long to visit the château, which was heavily restored in the 1960s after being burned by the Germans in World War II. Once you've viewed its temporary art expositions, you will have "done" Le Barroux. If you're in sightseeing hyperdrive, this is not the village for you. But if you settle into the simple family hotel Les Géraniums, perched on the hillside over the valley, you can dine on the terrace with seigneurial views and sleep to the sound of trickling fountains.

**CONTACT** Hôtel Les Géraniums, place de la Croix, 84330 Le Barroux, tel. 04-90-62-41-08, fax 04-90-62-56-48.

**DISTANCES** 16 km south of Vaison-la-Romaine, 34 km northeast of Avignon.

**FACILITIES** 22 rooms. Restaurant, bar. Closed Jan.–Feb.

**PRICES** Doubles 260–270 frs. Breakfast and dinner 250–270 frs/person.

**OPTIONS** There are hill towns clustered all around Mont Ventoux, each an aerie with a character of its own. **Venasque** (7C; 12 km southeast of Carpentras, 35 km northeast of Avignon), a tiny hilltop fortress-town, was once bishopric and capital of the county. There's a Merovingian baptistery behind its Église de Notre-Dame. At isolated **Crillon-le-Brave** (7B; 21 km southeast of Vaison), there's nothing but a luxury

hotel at its peak. (Hostellerie de Crillon le Brave, place de l'Église, 84410, tel. 04-90-65-61-61, fax 04-90-65-62-86, e-mail crillonbrave@relaischateaux.fr, on the Web at www.crillonbrave.com. 21 rooms, 3 suites. Restaurant, pool. Doubles 850–1,600 frs, suites 1,850–2,500 frs. Breakfast 85 frs.) **Séguret** (10 km southwest of Vaison) is topped with a medieval castle, a Romanesque church, and a 14th-century clock tower. And crouching against Mont Ventoux's wild northern flank, within shouting distance of the Drôme, **Brantes** (7B; 34 winding km east of Vaison) may be the most isolated and eerie of them all.

### HAUT-VAUCLUSE HIGHLIGHTS

This region was a major center of Roman culture, and important vestiges remain. At **Orange** (5B), there is a magnificent Roman theater, its stage wall still supporting a statue of Caesar Augustus; here the famous opera festival Les Chorégies d'Oranges takes place every July. There is also a massive Arc de Triomphe in central Orange, dating from 20 BC. In the very center of **Vaison-la-Romaine** (6B), two entire neighborhoods of Roman ruins stand exposed, including the foundations of villas, boutiques, baths, and a rank of flushing toilets.

# THE LUBERON

This may be the most fashionable region of Provence, and with good reason: To the north, south, and west of the Montagne du Luberon stretches some of the most picturesque and appealing country in the south of France. Arid but comfortably green, cloaked with thick pines and truffle oaks, striped with vineyards, peppered with olive groves and anchored with tile-roofed stone *mas* (farmhouses), it offers the quintessential Provençal landscape. The honey-colored stone hilltowns of Bonnieux, Ménerbes, Gordes, Lacoste, and Oppède strike a charming balance of bucolic-chic, with art galleries and trendy restaurants blending into the cobblestones and crumbling stucco. The Luberon is, of course, Peter Mayle country: It was of his house in Ménerbes that he first wrote the essays and sketches called *A Year in*

*Provence* and *Toujours Provence*. (Since that first burst of celebrity, he has quietly resettled in Lourmarin, on the Luberon's southern face.) The crowds of pleasure-seekers he in part inspired are thickest in high summer; spring and fall mix locals with visitors. But consider coming off-season, when a quieter rhythm returns to Luberon life and you, like Mayle, can walk the woods and explore the markets virtually undisturbed.

## SUNDAY MORNING ANTIQUES MARKET, L'ISLE-SUR-LA-SORGUE (6C)
*Trolling for Treasure, p. 54*

L'Isle-sur-la-Sorgue is a pleasant, low-key market town on the banks of the Sorgue, strategically placed between Avignon and the western slopes of the Luberon. Its streets are interlaced with canals and branches of the Sorgue, whose waters once drove the wheels of silk, paper, oil, grain, and leather mills. Today these wheels—eight of them—turn idly, heavy with moss, adding to the charm of the winding streets. The name l'Isle-sur-la-Sorgue has become inextricably mixed with the cult of antiquing. Not only does the Sunday market offer an embarrassment of riches at temporary stands, but shops—indeed, entire malls—of antiques draw upmarket collectors all week long. While the food stands and arts and crafts hold forth along the Avenue de la Libération, the antiquaires hold Sunday squatters' rights from the Place Gambetta up the length of Avenue des 4 Otages.

**CONTACT** Office du Tourisme de l'Isle-sur-la-Sorgue, Place de l'Église, 84800, tel. 04–90–38–04–78, fax 04–90–38–35–43.

**DISTANCES** 25 km east of Avignon.

**OPTIONS Mas de Cure Bourse:** For a real taste of the countryside, base yourself at this 18th-century stagecoach inn on landscaped grounds southwest of town. Sunday dinner is a tradition here, served on rustic ceramic platters under the vaulted ceilings and daubed beams, with the massive family hound standing guard. Rooms have hand-painted Provençal furniture, ochre walls, bright printed cotton fabrics and, of course, antiques and linens gleaned from nearby anti-

quaires. Route de Caumont, 84800 l'Isle-sur-la-Sorgue, tel. 04–90–38–16–58, fax 04–90–38–52–31. 13 rooms. Restaurant, pool. Doubles 400–600 frs, breakfast 50 frs. Closed three weeks in Nov. and first two weeks in Jan.

## RURAL HOLIDAY RENTAL, THE LUBERON (7–9D)
*Living the Gîte Life, p. 42*

Europeans have long enjoyed the leisure and privacy of renting country gîtes during their relatively long vacations, but Americans—eager to cover maximum ground abroad—often overlook the advantages of staying put. Gîtes de France is a nationwide rental network for rural vacation homes. They are, by definition, outside city centers and usually rich in regional character; many of them are restored farmhouses and old village *bastides* (country houses). Owners are nearly always on-site or next door, offering a personal welcome and advice, then fading comfortably into the background. All gîtes are rented for one week at a time, Saturday afternoon to the next Saturday morning. Choose the *département* where you want to base yourself, then contact that region's satellite office. You can order a catalog, study maps, and make a reservation by phone or fax. You must give them a 25% down payment with your reservation, then the rest when you return the contract, one month before your visit.

**CONTACT** Gîtes de France-Alpes de Haute-Provence, Rond-Point du 11 novembre, 04000 Digne-les-Bains, tel. 04–92–31–52–39, fax 04–92–32–32–63. Includes Forcalquier, Manosque, and Moustiers-Ste-Marie.

Gîtes de France-Bouches-du-Rhône, Domaine-du-Vergon, B.P. 26, 13370 Mallemort, tel. 04–90–59–49–39, fax 04–90–59–16–75. Includes Marseille, Aix, St-Rémy-de-Provence, Les Baux, Cassis, Arles, and Stes-Maries.

Gîtes de France-Var, Rond-point du 4/12/74, B.P. 215. tel. 04–94–50–93–93, fax 04–94–50–93–90. Includes Draguignan, Cotignac, and Lorgues.

Gîtes de France-Vaucluse, La Balance, place Campana, B.P. 164. 84008 Avignon cedex, tel. 04–90–85–45–00, fax 04–90–85–88–49. Includes Avignon, Vaison-la-Romaine,

Carpentras, l'Isle-sur-la-Sorgue, and Roussillon.

**FACILITIES** Gîtes de France sets strict comfort standards, rated by *épis* or ears of corn and enforced with equipment lists, right down to the number of can openers. Three épis, for example, assures you of a washing machine and use of a telephone. Bed linens and towels are not included, but often can be rented on request. Four épis is the highest rating available; at that level, you may get a swimming pool.

**PRICES** Gîtes vary widely in price, but perfectly clean, moderate accommodations can cost a fraction of hotel rates. Most one- and two-bedrooms start at 1,500 frs per week; the larger converted farmhouses can cost 3,000–4,000 frs; the most luxurious prestige gîtes with swimming pools ask up to 7,000 frs per week. Gîte capacities are strictly enforced; that is, four-person lodgings cannot, without violating insurance coverage, accommodate six.

**OPTIONS** Getting around while based at a rural gîte requires wheels, and if you're investing more than two weeks in the barefoot life, then consider leasing a car from Kemwel. For a minimum of 17 days you can have a new Peugeot, VAT-free, with full insurance coverage (also tax-free), unlimited mileage and 24-hour emergency roadside assistance. Pickup points in Provence include Avignon and Marseille airport. For information contact 800/678–0678 or the Kemwel Web site: www.kemwel.com.

**OCHRE VEIN, ROUSSILLON TO APT, VAUCLUSE** (7–8D)
*Luxe in Terra, p. 50*

A rich vein of ochre runs through the earth between Roussillon (7D), Gargas (7D), and Rustrel (8C), occasionally breaking the surface in technicolor displays of russet, garnet, and flaming orange. Roussillon itself is a mineral showcase, perched above a pocket of red-rock canyonlands that are reflected in the stuccoes applied on every building in town. At the edge of town, on the grounds of the Usine Mathieu, a former ochre mine/processing plant, the Conservatoire des Ochres et Pigments Appliqués offers visitors a total-immersion experience (sometimes literally) in the rich dust and pastes of local ochre. You may simply take a tour and learn how the raw material is extracted, rinsed and baked; or you may sign up for two-day hands-on workshops. Children may spend a half-day making paints from raw pigments or explore the vestiges of the old factory. And on special occasions you may take a tour to the neighboring quarry at Gargas, where massive chunks of raw material are extracted from high, pure-ochre cliffs.

**CONTACT** Barbara and Mathieu Barrois, OKHRA/Conservatoire des Ochres et Pigments Appliqués, 84220 Roussillon, tel./fax 04–90–05–66–69. La Societé des Ochres de France at Apt permits tours of the factory the first Wednesday of the month or by appointment; either tour is arranged by the Conservatoire at Roussillon. It is a working industrial supplier and does not sell ochre in small quantities; these may be had at the Conservatoire. Impasse des Ochriers, 84401 Apt, tel. 04–90–74–63–82, fax 04–90–74–46–75.

**DISTANCES** Apt is 52 km east of Avignon. Roussillon is 10 km northwest of Apt.

**OPTIONS Ma Maison:** There are several acceptable mid-level hotels in the town of Roussillon, but if your ochre-touring has awakened your eye for the painterly and the beautifully composed, Ma Maison is worth heading down into the valley. On artistically landscaped grounds, this gracious old stone *mas* has been transformed into a serene and stylish bed-and-breakfast. Two French artists host your stay, and their sojourn in California clearly has informed their laid-back, barefoot ways. Quartier Les Devens, 84220 Roussillon, tel. 04–90–05–74–17, fax 04–90–05–74–63. Doubles 450–650 frs.

**PROVENÇAL MARKETS** (6–9D)
*A Moveable Feast, p. 74*

The Provençal market is a deeply ingrained part of daily life throughout Provence, with one in a nearby village every day of the week. Each market transforms itself to reflect something organic and intrinsic to the village itself: The cafés that border the square or esplanade where the market holds forth become market cafés, where merchants drink their

morning rosé and crunch down a sausage-stuffed baguette. The nearest bakery becomes part of the ensemble of temporary stands, the last stop after your basket is full. And any day of the week if you ask directions to the museum or tourist office, a native may unthinkingly gesture, "There, over there where the market is," when the market won't be there until next Tuesday. You'll find markets all across Provence, not just in the Luberon, but also throughout the Vaucluse, the Var, and the Bouches-du-Rhône.

## BEST VAUCLUSE MARKET DAYS

**Sunday:** Coustellet, l'Isle-sur-la-Sorgue, **Monday:** Cadanet, Cavaillon, **Tuesday:** Vaison-la-Romaine, **Wednesday:** Malaucène, Sault, **Thursday:** Orange, La Motte d'Aigues (mid-June–Sept. 6–10 PM), **Friday:** Bonnieux, Carpentras, Pertuis, **Saturday:** Apt, Pernes-les-Fontaines

**OPTIONS** In the *département* Bouches-du-Rhône, there are also lively markets at Aubagne (Tues.), St-Rémy (Wed.), Aix (Tues., Thurs. and Sat.), and Arles (Sat.).

## LUBERON HIGHLIGHTS

Scattered through the countryside, mysterious stone hovels called *bories* have deliciously vague histories. The first were built in eons past by Celto-Ligurians, and their primeval form was mimicked and reproduced through the 18th century. A complete village of bories has been reconstructed on ancient foundations outside the hilltown of **Gordes** (7C). Four km north of Gordes, the magnificently austere **Abbaye de Sénanque** (7C) rises in borie-like cylinders and domes over fields of lavender. Five km as the crow flies west of Gordes (but accessed by lovely circuitous hill roads), the **Fontaine de Vaucluse** (6C) wells out of the earth at the foot of a vertiginous limestone cliff, then spills in torrents through its quaint mill town. The hilltowns of **Bonnieux, Ménerbes,** and **Oppède** (7D) have a character of their own, but Lacoste features the jagged ruins of the Château de Sade, where the famous Marquis practiced and recorded his shocking exploits—before his mother-in-law turned him in to the authorities.

# ALPES-DE-HAUTE-PROVENCE

As you rise above the arid plains of southern Provence the hills grow steeper, the air takes on an edge of chill, and the warm ochre stuccoes that grace Vaucluse and Var houses are replaced by gray stone: This is Haute-Provence, the spare, wind-scrubbed mountainous landscape that joins coastal Provence to the Alps. Its western flank blanketed with lavender fields, its south carved into canyons by the roaring Verdon, this region mounts inexorably into high-altitude greenery and opens to the north on a skyline of snow-capped peaks. Its people remain aloof to the coast, as battened down against day-tripping tourism as they are against the harsh northerly winds. All the more room for serious exploration, then: Space to wander, to climb, to contemplate the brooding landscape.

## HIKING THE SENTIER MARTEL, GORGES DU VERDON (12D)
*Trial by Trail, p. 36*

If you're testing your mettle on the Sentier Martel, plan on at least six hours' walk from the departure point—le Châlet de la Maline, below La Palud—to the Couloir Samson, beneath the appropriately named Point Sublime. Leave your car at the Couloir Samson parking lot, then have a taxi pick you up (arranged the night before) and drop you at your departure point. Carry at least a liter of water and wear sturdy hiking shoes with lug soles: The limestone stays damp and slippery year round, and the gravel slides are ankle-busting rough. A flashlight is imperative for the two ink-black tunnels, one of them 2,198 feet long. And no dogs or children under six years old. Having second thoughts? You can, of course, take in spectacular views from the top at roadside overlooks along both sides of the Gorges du Verdon. The Corniche Sublime follows the D71 from Comps to Aiguine along breathtaking switchbacks. The north-bank drive from Moustiers to Castellane (D952) takes in equally memorable perspectives.

**CONTACTS** Verdon Accueil (Verdon Welcome) provides tourist information at Castellane (04120 Castellane, rue Nationale, tel. 04–92–83–67–36). For maps and information on lodging, contact the tourist offices in Moustiers (04360 Moustiers, tel. 04–92–74–67–84, fax 04–92–74–60–65) and at La Palud (Cour du Château, 04120 La Palud-sur-Verdon, tel. 04–92–77–32–02, fax 04–92–77–30–87). For taxis out of La Palud, call 04–92–77–38–20, 04–92–83–65–34, or 04–92–83–65–38.

**DISTANCES** Moustiers-Ste-Marie is 67 km northwest of Draguignan. La Palud-sur-Verdon is 26 km southwest of Castellane.

**OPTIONS Bastide de Moustiers:** Pamper yourself before and after your hike at celebrity chef Alain Ducasse's country retreat at the pretty village of Moustiers. The airy, modern rooms dressed in Provençal fabrics, the hedge-hidden swimming pool, and the famous regional cuisine justify the investment. Chemin de Quinson, 04360 Moustiers, tel. 04–92–70–47–47, fax 04–92–70–47–48, e-mail to bastide@i2m.fr or chatotel@chatotel.com, on the Web at www.bastide-moustiers.i2m.fr or www.chatotel.com. 11 rooms, 1 suite. Restaurant, air conditioning, pool. Doubles 850–1,470 frs, suite 1,480–1,700 frs.

### THE TRANSHUMANCE, ALPES-DE-HAUTE-PROVENCE (12 B–D)

*Heading for the Hills, p. 32*

Pioneers in the revival of the mass migration of Provençal sheep into the greenery of the Alps, Christian, Christine, and Bernard Menud drive their herds yearly from St-Julien-de-Montagnier, near Manosque, to the Col d'Allos, accompanied by professional shepherds-in-training and a gaggle of fans and friends. To witness their *troupeau*—or any others—passing through, base yourself in late June at one of the many villages along their time-honored route. (The Menut family sheep are branded MC.) Herd after herd, sometimes two or three in one day, flow through the villages of Comps-sur-Artuby, Castellane, St-Julien-sur-Verdon, St-André-les-Alpes, Colmars, and Allos. Leaving behind the dry stubble of the Var, they move up the highways and backroads, led by a

dozen or so guides with fluorescent vests and whips to crack above the dumb beasts' heads. To avoid the heat of the day (the sheep refuse to walk in high sun), man and beast arise at 4 AM, walk until late morning, eat and rest all afternoon, and hit the road again at 5 PM . . . to walk until nearly midnight. They move slowly, stopping to graze at every patch of greenery, and must squeeze aside to let traffic pass. To see this epic rite of passage, get an early start and ask at cafés and tourist offices: They'll know when the next one's coming through.

**CONTACTS** Office du Tourisme de Castellane, rue Nationale, B.P. 8, 04120, tel. 04–92–83–61–14, fax 04–92–83–76–89. Office du Tourisme de Colmars-les-Alpes, place Joseph-Girieud, 04370, tel. 04–92–83–41–92 , fax 04–92–83–52–31.

**DISTANCES** Castellane is 82 km from Draguignan. Comps is 32 km from Draguignan. Colmars is 132 km from Draguignan.

**OPTIONS Grand Hôtel Bain:** The landmark stopover for transalpine stage coaches still provides shelter and a hot meal for travelers through Comps-sur-Artuby, and has been run by the Bain family, fathers and sons, since 1737. Clean, modernized rooms, cozy salons and a panoramic dining room draw hikers, families, and epicures. Off D21 in the village center, 83840, tel. 04–94–76–90–06, fax 04–94–76–92–24. 18 rooms. Restaurant, terrace café, TV. Doubles 265–285 frs. Breakfast 38 frs. **Nouvel Hôtel du Commerce:** At the foot of Castellane's high chalk cliff, this offers comfortable, simple rooms and cut-above Provençal cooking. Place de l'Église, 04120 Castellane, tel. 04–92–83–61–00, fax 04–92–83–72–82. 42 rooms. Restaurant, terrace café. Doubles 315–360 frs.

### CUTTING WILD LAVENDER, ABOVE FORCALQUIER (9C)

*The Essence of the Matter, p. 72*

Like Holland's May tulips, the lavender of Haute-Provence is in its glory only once a year: the last two weeks of July, when for miles the landscape breaks out in saturated shades of purple. You'll see it throughout the region east of the Rhône and north of the Luberon, but production and distillation is particularly concentrated around Forcalquier, where Monique Claessens sells her herbal wares. Look for her stand at the Monday market from 8 AM until noon.

**CONTACT** Monique Claessens' headquarters stands on a hillside above Mane: Head northeast on N100 to Forcalquier, then take D950 northwest to Ybourgues and turn uphill left at Saint-Lambert. Here, at her communal farm, you can find her alchemy in full swing. By appointment only. Tel. 04–92–73–06–76, fax 04–92–73–04–14.

For maps of colorful drives, addresses of distilleries, lodging and dining suggestions, and background information on lavender production, contact the global organization called **Les Routes de la Lavande**, 2 av. de Venterol, B.P. 36, 26111 Nyons cedex, tel. 04–75–26–65–91, fax 04–75–26–32–67.

**DISTANCES** 75 km from Avignon, 42 km from Sisteron.

**OPTIONS** To literally immerse yourself in lavender, head north to Eygalayes in the Drôme, where you can take a lavender cure in Gaby and Jacques Laurent's bed-and-breakfast. Lavender spa-baths, aromatic saunas and essential oil massages put you in top form to pursue the biking and hiking options in the surrounding countryside, and to enjoy the table d'hôte dinners. Gaby and Jacques Laurent, La Forges Sainte-Marie, 26560 Eygalayes, tel./fax 04–75–28–42–77. Doubles with breakfast 270 frs. Treatments 50 frs per session.

**ALPES DE HAUTE-PROVENCE HIGHLIGHTS**
**Moustiers-Sainte-Marie** (11D) is one of the most famous centers of faïence in France, creating milky-glazed pottery painted with lacy grotesques in blue and yellow. Explore its dozen or so modern artisans' shops, and study the forebears in the Musée de la Faïence, place du Presbytère, 04360 Moustiers-Sainte-Marie, tel. 04–92–74–6–64. The symbiotic by-product of lavender is, of course, honey, and this aromatic sweet is sold at boutiques and roadside stands throughout the region. If you're eager to dig deeper into Haute-Provence history and culture, spend a day at the Conservatoire du Patrimoine Ethnologique de Haute-Provence, a hybrid of museum, library, bookstore, and con-

templative retreat in an ancient stone priory. Prieuré de Salagon, 04300 Mane/Forcalquier, tel 04–92–75–70–50, fax 04–92–75–70–51.

# HAUT VAR

Behind the A8 autoroute that slices across Provence and its Mediterranean coastline, hills rake sharply upward on a plateau that rises inexorably towards the Alps. Palm trees give way to wind-twisted pines, truffle oaks, and resinous herbs that crackle underfoot. Glamorous resorts are guarded by high hill-town fortresses that have watched over the coastline from the heights since the days of Moorish invasions. This quiet region, relatively unspoiled, is called the Haut Var—the highlands of the département of the Var, which stretches from Cassis to Cannes. Far from the fast-track Côte d'Azur scene south of the freeway, life putters on at an easy pace here. This is the region to explore in early springtime, when the gentle sun is welcomed at sidewalk cafés, and in the fall when the forests burnish with autumn colors. Driving from village to village, through vineyards and to the tops of fortified hilltowns, you'll know Provence at its mellowest.

## CÔTES DE PROVENCE GRAPE HARVEST, LORGUES (12F)

*Autumn Bacchanalia, p. 46*

To really experience the *vendange* (grape harvest) first hand, the only way to go is to participate. Every autumn, enthusiastic pickers migrate to the vineyards, volunteers mingling with hourly laborers, farmers with intellectuals who enjoy reaping what later they will savor. In this user-friendly region, several vineyards offer visitors a hands-on experience of the harvest, complete with lodging and occasional alfresco feasts. If you want to sign up, be flexible: Everything depends on the grapes. Ripening is keyed to the year's weather, and when the sugar content reaches critical mass, it's time to pick. Rain turns the furrows to masses of mud; a heat wave hastens the process to urgency. Plan to be in the region in mid-September, and allow a two-week margin; from the 12th through the 30th, different varietals reach their peak and are gathered post-haste. Bring a raincoat and disposable shoes or rubber boots. And dress in layers: You'll want to strip down when the sun hits high noon. Sometimes workers eat a communal lunch; more often they bring a *casse-croûte* (bag lunch). The fruit course is always included: The grapes are there for the gorging. And last year's vintage is readily available to quench your thirst.

**CONTACT** For general information on the region and visitor-friendly vendanges, contact the Comité Départemental du Tourisme du Var, 1 bd. Foch, B.P. 99, 83003 Draguignan cedex, tel. 04-94-50-55-50, fax 04-94-50-55-51.

**DISTANCES** 13 km west of Draguignan, 42 km northwest of Fréjus.

**OPTIONS** In Côte de Provence rosé country southwest of Draguignan, two vignobles offer participation programs for the *vendange*. **Domaine Saint Jean-Baptiste:** Outside Lorgues, this is a small, friendly estate offering individual participation in the vendange and bed-and-breakfast accommodation in the family farmhouse. Individuals or small groups can spend a day (250 frs per person) learning, picking, and studying the nuances of vinification. Lodging should be booked well in advance. There's also a three-day package for participation in the *vendange,* including grape-cutting sessions, two group lunches, bed-and-breakfast, and observation-training on winemaking. The price is 1,100 frs per couple in a double room. Brigitte Grivet, Domaine Saint Jean-Baptiste, 1525 route des Arcs, 83510 Lorgues, tel. 04-94-73-71-11, fax 04-94-73-26-91, e-mail to jean-baptiste@caves-particulieres.com. Doubles 275 frs, including breakfast. **Château de St-Martin:** Resident aristocrats run this glorious old estate outside Taradeau. Here groups of six or more can spend a day picking, learning about the wine-making process, and tasting the house products; the next year the fruits of your labors—a bottle of wine with a personalized label—will be shipped to you. 240 frs per person,

from September 15–30. Advance reservation and 50% deposit required. Contact Adeline de Barry, Château de St-Martin, 83460 Taradeau, tel. 04-94-73-02-01, fax 04-94-73-12-36.

## COTIGNAC (11F)
*Plane Trees, Pétanque, Pastis, p. 22*

To experience Cotignac at its mellow best, base yourself directly on the cours Gambetta in the landmark hotel Lou Calen. Renovated to the roots under Swedish ownership, it features state-of-the-art bathrooms and a chic Provençal decor. The restaurant tables spill onto a landscaped garden courtyard with pool.

**CONTACT** Hôtel Lou Calen, cours Gambetta, 83570, Cotignac, tel. 04-94-04-60-40, fax 04-94-04-76-64.

**DISTANCES** 36 km west of Draguignan, 75 km northwest of Fréjus.

**FACILITIES** 12 rooms, 3 suites. Restaurant, pool.

**PRICES** Although unavailable at press time, post-renovation price are sure to be steep, appropriate to the landmark hotel's four-star standing.

**OPTIONS** Cotignac's ever-active pétanque court lies just across the cours Gambetta from Lou Calen. Here the pétanque club calls itself La Boule Fleurie, and the president himself, Adrien Garcin, holds forth from the observation benches on a daily basis. When you're played out, stretch your legs by climbing the face of La Roche, the vertiginous cliff that shelters the town. It's riddled with caves that served as observation posts for military guards.

**LODGING OPTIONS** To make the most personal contact with the friendly people of Cotignac, stay in one of the many chambres-d'hôte (bed and breakfasts) in and around town; the tourist office provides listings (rue Bonaventure, Cotignac 83570. Tel 04-94-04-61-87). The fine old bastide of the Domaine de Nestuby lies in a private vineyard four km out of town, toward Brignoles. Here Nathalie and Jean-

François Roubaud offer meals and tastings of their own Côtes-de-Provence. Tel 04–94–04–60–02, fax 04–94–04–79–22. 4 rooms, table d'hôte dinners, wine tastings. Doubles 350 frs.

## HAUT VAR HIGHLIGHTS

Thirty km southwest of Draguignan, the **Abbaye du Thoronet** (11F), built in the 12th century by Cistercian monks, is one of the finest examples of Romanesque architecture in Provence. Its pure austerity of line was a reaction, in part, to the perceived extravagance of the Cluny abbey in Burgundy. The **Château d'Entrecasteaux** (11F), 9 km east of Cotignac, is a 17th-century structure with slender, refined lines; tour the gardens, kitchen, and furnished salons. The hilltop fortified village of **Tourtour** (11E), 28 km northeast of Draguignan, has galleries, boutiques, and cafés—and wraparound views of the Haut Var.

# AIX AND THE MARSEILLE COAST

This easternmost chunk of the département known as Bouches-du-Rhône (literally, "Mouths of the Rhône") may be sideswiped by the mistral winds that sweep down the Rhône to its west or may be cooled by Mediterranean breezes that flutter in from its coastline, but its arid, sunbaked landscape has a personality all its own—rugged, rocky, fiercely beautiful. All this natural beauty comes neatly framed between two sophisticated cities, diametric opposites in spirit and form: chic, gracious Aix, all shady boulevards and café life; and feisty Marseille, vigorous, tough, exotic, and redolent of the cultures that ship into its ancient ports. Between lies Marcel Pagnol country in the hills around Aubagne, within runout distance of the coastal *calanques* at Cassis. Life hums on year-round here, with spikes of cultural activity during Aix's summer music festival and Marseille's winter opera-and-theater season. Farmer's markets (and fish markets, too) flourish all year, and Christmas takes on a southern sparkle in both Aix and Marseille's embarrassment of shopping riches.

## IN SEARCH OF THE PERFECT BOUILLABAISSE, MARSEILLE (7–8G)
*Mediterranean Melting Pot, p. 18*

To experience Marseille from its heart, make your headquarters the comfortable, charming Hotel Mercure-Beauvau, directly on the Vieux Port. From a port-side balcony in this 1816 landmark you'll take in the full romantic perspective of Marseille's hill-flanked harbor, its fortresses, and neo-Byzantine monuments.

**CONTACT** Hotel Mercure-Beauvau-Vieux-Port, 4 rue Beauvau, 13001 Marseille, tel. 04–91–54–91–00, fax 04–91–54–15–76, e-mail to H1293@accord-hotels.com or mercure-beauvau@ provencetourism.com. For U.S. reservations, call 800/MER-CURE.

**DISTANCES** 30 km from Aix-en-Provence, 15 km from Aubagne, 22 km from Cassis.

**FACILITIES** 71 rooms, 1 suite. Bar, breakfast buffet. Ask for port-side room.

**PRICES** Double 660–780 frs. Chopin suite 1,600 frs. Breakfast buffet 67 frs.

**OTHER OPTIONS Hotel Alizé:** Also fronting the port, but for smaller budgets, this hotel has simple, modern rooms. 35 quai des Belges, 13001, tel. 04–91–33–66–97, fax 04–91–54–80–06, on the web at www.alize-hotel.com. 37 rooms. Double 335–395 frs. Breakfast 35 frs. **Hotel Hermès:** Around the corner from the quai du Port, this hostelry has tidy, modular rooms. Ask for one of the three fifth-floor rooms with enclosed balconies overlooking the port, or book the honeymoon rooftop double with crow's-nest views of the water. 2 rue Bonneterie, 13002 Marseille, tel. 04–96–11–63–63, fax 04–96–11–63–64. Double 300–350 frs, rooftop *nuptiale* double 470 frs. **Chez Fonfon:** For the perfect bouillabaisse, take a taxi to the Vallon des Auffes, one of Marseille's myriad charming fishing ports, a tiny village within city limits. Here Chez Fonfon is a local institution for bouillabaisse with all the theatrical flourish it requires, against a film-set backdrop. 140 rue du Vallon des Auffes, tel. 04–91–52–14–38. Closed Sun. dinner.

## THE CALANQUES BETWEEN MARSEILLE AND CASSIS (8G)
*Castaway in Paradise, p. 14*

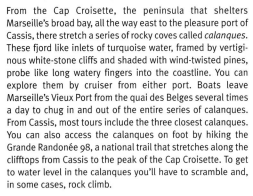

From the Cap Croisette, the peninsula that shelters Marseille's broad bay, all the way east to the pleasure port of Cassis, there stretch a series of rocky coves called *calanques*. These fjord like inlets of turquoise water, framed by vertiginous white-stone cliffs and shaded with wind-twisted pines, probe like long watery fingers into the coastline. You can explore them by cruiser from either port. Boats leave Marseille's Vieux Port from the quai des Belges several times a day to chug in and out of the entire series of calanques. From Cassis, most tours include the three closest calanques. You can also access the calanques on foot by hiking the Grande Randonée 98, a national trail that stretches along the clifftops from Cassis to the peak of the Cap Croisette. To get to water level in the calanques you'll have to scramble and, in some cases, rock climb.

**CONTACT** From Marseille, the Groupement des Armateurs Cotiers Marseillais offers *mini-croisières* (mini-cruises) to the entire ensemble of calanques, lasting about four hours for 120 frs/person. If the weather is iffy, call in advance to confirm. 1 quai des Belges, 13001 Marseille, tel. 04–91–55–50–09, fax 04–91–55–60–23. Their Web site offers seasonal schedules: www.answeb.net/gacm. From Cassis, the maritime company called La Visite des Calanques maintains several boats that leave the Quai des Baux (opposite the port restaurants) at least twice daily even off-season; buy your tickets at the dock. 1 bis rue Gervais, 13260 Cassis, tel. 04–91–06–99–35.

**DISTANCES** Calanques, ports, and *anses* (inlets) stretch the entire distance of 25 km from Marseille to Cassis.

**OPTIONS Le Petit Nice:** Though it's just around the corner from busy downtown Marseille, this luxurious hotel lodges guests on a clifftop over the crashing surf and serves, not incidentally, some of the finest seafood in the south. Anses de Maldormé, corniche J-F Kennedy, 13007 Marseille, tel. 04–91–59–25–92, fax 04–91–59–28–08. 15 rooms. Restaurant, air-conditioning, pool. Doubles 1,000–1,500 frs.

**Jardin d'Émile:** In Cassis, this intimate and charming lodging sits back from the waterfront in a pine-shaded niche. Half the rooms angle toward the cape and coast. Plage du Bestouan, 13260 Cassis, tel. 04–42–01–80–55, fax 04–42–01–80–70. 7 rooms. Restaurant. Doubles 400–550 frs Nov.–Mar., 450–650 frs Apr.–Oct. Breakfast 58 frs. **Baie des Singes:** For a day's indulgence dining, diving, and lounging in a rocky cove on the Cap Croisette south of Marseille, this lovely escape rents mattresses, lounge chairs, and showers to diners for an additional 50 frs. Anses des Croisettes, Les Goudes, tel. 04–91–73–68–87.

## AIX-EN-PROVENCE TO MONTAGNE STE-VICTOIRE (8–9F)
*Tracing Cézanne, p. 8*

To trace the master's footsteps base yourself in Aix's center. The extravagantly lovely Villa Gallici offers sumptuous lodging on the hillside neighboring Cézanne's studio. Rooms mix painterly fabrics and local ceramics, and the formal Mediterranean gardens make for idyllic breakfasts and pooltime. Just over the hill, the Atelier Cézanne is open to the public April through September daily from 10 to noon and 2:30 to 6. From October through March, it is open daily from 10 to noon and 2 to 5. There are guided tours Wednesdays and Saturdays at 10 and 3 (English on request).

**CONTACT** Villa Gallici, avenue de la Violette, 13100 Aix, tel. 04–42–23–29–23, fax 04–42–96–30–45, e-mail to gallici@relaischateaux.fr or resarc@relaischateaux.fr, on the web at www.relaischateaux.fr.

**DISTANCES** 30 km from Marseille, 80 km from Avignon.

**FACILITIES** 18 rooms, 4 suites. Air-conditioning, television, safes. Garden, pool. On-site restaurant and more formal Le Clos de la Violette, 100 yards away.

**PRICES** Apr.–Oct. doubles 1,350–2,650 frs, suites 2,650–3,050 frs. Nov.–Mar. doubles 1,000–2,150 frs, suites 2,150–2,500 frs.

**OTHER OPTIONS Relais Ste-Victoire:** A more contemplative country experience near Cézanne's beloved Montagne Ste-Victoire can be had at this simple lodging (and top-drawer restaurant) near Beaurecueil, 10 km east of Aix. You'll wake in red rock and pine country, and it's an easy jaunt to seek out the artist's favorite views of the mountain. Take D17 out of Aix, direction Le Tholonet; turn right on D46 into Beaurecueil. 13100 Beaurecueil, tel. 04–42–66–94–98, fax 04–42–66–85–96. 10 rooms. Restaurant, pool. Double 400–800frs.

## CHRISTMASTIME, AUBAGNE (8G)
*Noël, Noël!, p. 64*

At the foot of the rounded peak of the Garlaban, Aubagne was birthplace to Provence's greatest raconteur, the writer and filmmaker Marcel Pagnol, and this low-key market town still retains a folklorique sense of Old Provence. *Santonniers,* the craftsmen who mold, paint, and dress the ubiquitous terra-cotta figures, first came to Aubagne from Marseille, drawn by the fine local clay. Their craft became a form of storytelling, with a cast of familiar characters appearing in every Christmas crèche, village personalities that have, over the years, taken on a life of their own. Though today santonniers work throughout Provence, Aubagne has become a kind of focal point for the craft, with a dozen artisans based in town and another dozen scattered nearby. Some have achieved major status in the field: Daniel Scatturo, who specializes in live-portrait santons and figures of Pagnol characters (including Yves Montand and Gérard Depardieu from Pagnol's beloved *Jean de Florette*) has been granted the prestigious classification of Meilleur Ouvrier de France ("Best Artisan of France"). Scaturro has a *salle d'exposition* on the edge of town (20A av. de Verdun, tel. 04–42–84–33–29) as well as a tiny demonstration studio in the old town, where his sons carry on the family tradition.

**CONTACTS** For a booklet with directions to the area's santonniers, contact the Maison du Tourisme du Pays d'Aubagne, Avenue Antide Boyer, 13400 Aubagne, tel. 04–42–03–49–98, fax 04–42–03–83–62, e-mail to aubagnetour@aubagne.com, on the Web at www.aubagne.com. Every December on the cours Foch, the Foire aux santons et à la céramique features stands of santonniers showing their best Christmas figurines, all surrounding a massive all-santon Christmas crèche.

**DISTANCES** Aubagne is 16 km east of Marseille, 28 km south of Aix.

**OPTIONS Hostellerie de la Source:** As Aubagne isn't a tourist center, lodging in town is mainly freeway-exit stuff. For a slightly more charming experience, drive three km north of town to St-Pierre-les Aubagne, where you'll find this 17th-century *bastide* with a pool, tennis court, and manicured grounds. 13400 Aubagne, tel. 04–42–04–09–19, fax 04–42–04–58–72. 24 rooms, 1 suite. Restaurant, bar, pool, tennis court, garden. Doubles 450 frs.

**AIX AND THE MARSEILLE COAST HIGHLIGHTS** In **Aix** (8E), the Musée Granet displays eight Cézanne paintings in his former École de Dessin (Art School). In the Cathédrale St-Sauveur, there's a Merovingian baptistery and a magnificent 15th-century triptych by Nicolas Froment; it is only open for viewing once a week (Tuesdays from 3 to 4) to avoid light damage. In **Marseille** (8G), visit the Musée d'Histoire de Marseille (Museum of Marseille History) and the Musée d'Archéologie Mediterranéenne (Museum of Mediterranean Archeology) in the old seafarer's neighborhood Le Panier. In **Aubagne** (8G), be sure to take in a market day: Tuesday's is the biggest, while Saturday and Sunday feature local, pesticide-free farm products. **Cassis** (8G) is famous for the wine that bears its name, especially its crisp, fruity white—just the thing to wash down a platter of local *oursins* (sea urchins) and a spicy bouillabaisse. Vineyards with tasting caves surround the port town.

Author Nancy Coons, who has been writing out of Europe since 1987 (*European Travel & Life, The Wall Street Journal, National Geographic Traveler*), could have made up all these Escapes and stayed home with her family in Lorraine, sipping pastis, watching Pagnol videos and reading Peter Mayle. But already having put down roots in the land of cigales and plane trees during years of research for other Fodor's projects, she went to the other extreme. She picked grapes in the Var, scuffed shin-deep through ochre dust, rode horseback in the Camargue, set up housekeeping in nine rural gîtes, hiked the Sentier Martel (once each way), and trudged 180 km behind 2,500 clamorous sheep.

Photographer Owen Franken, having survived a close call with a career as an astrophysicist, (MIT '68), gave up hard news for food and wine and travel and moved to Paris for the oysters. He has published in *National Geographic Traveler, Travel & Leisure, Gourmet, Food & Wine, Saveur, The New York Times,* and other publications worldwide. Franken is crazy about Provence and will go there with the slightest excuse, "We have run out of olive oil" being the most common.